Reflections

In the care of the Good Shepherd
Meditations on Psalm 23

Iain D Campbell

DayOne

© Day One Publications 2009
First Edition 2009

British Library Cataloguing in Publication Data available

ISBN 978-1-84625-175-7

Published by Day One Publications
Ryelands Road, Leominster, HR6 8NZ

☎ 01568 613 740
FAX: 01568 611 473
email—sales@dayone.co.uk
web site—www.dayone.co.uk
North American e-mail—usasales@dayone.co.uk
North American web site—www.dayonebookstore.com

Cover designed by Wayne McMaster and printed by Gutenberg Press, Malta

Dedication
To my good friends, John and Angela Tweeddale
and their daughter Amelia, whose fellowship in
the gospel has been an inspiration. John: may your
ministry beginning in Pittsburgh be mightily blessed
under the sovereign grace of the Chief Shepherd.

Endorsements

In this devotional treatment of Psalm 23, Dr Iain D. Campbell describes the onset of spiritual life in Christians, their varied progress as followers of Jesus the Good Shepherd, and their final destiny in his presence for ever. By tracing the metaphor of shepherding throughout the Old and New Testaments, the author makes insightful use of this rich imagery as it describes the work of Christ as the Companion, Leader, Provider and Protector of his people. The book is written by one who functions as an under-shepherd of the Saviour and who is aware of the spiritual needs and desires of his flock, and this experience is very much to the fore throughout the work. Further, the activities of Jesus are described in such a straightforward devotional manner that makes the book a joy to read. It is a book suitable for the heart as well as for the mind.

Revd Dr Malcolm Maclean, Minister, Greyfriars Free Church, Inverness, Scotland

Iain D. Campbell's exposition of Psalm 23 is masterful, both exegetically and pastorally. Reminiscent of the late Douglas MacMillan's work on this psalm, Dr Campbell's adds significantly to our appreciation of the psalm; indeed, under his guidance we are led to behold new vistas of greener pastures and still waters. Sure-footed expository genius of a rare kind.

Derek Thomas, John E. Richards Professor of Theology, Reformed Theological Seminary (Jackson); Minister of Teaching, First Presbyterian Church, Jackson, Mississippi, USA; and Editorial Director, Reformation21.org

Contents

Psalm 23

The Lord is my shepherd; I shall not want.
   He makes me lie down in green pastures.
He leads me beside still waters.
   He restores my soul.
He leads me in paths of righteousness
   for his name's sake.

Even though I walk through the valley
   of the shadow of death,
   I will fear no evil,
for you are with me;
   your rod and your staff,
   they comfort me.

You prepare a table before me
   in the presence of my enemies;
you anoint my head with oil;
   my cup overflows.
Surely goodness and mercy shall follow me
   all the days of my life,
and I shall dwell in the house of the Lord
   for ever.

Introduction

These reflections on Psalm 23 began life as a series of sermons in Back Free Church, Isle of Lewis, Scotland, during summer 2008. I am grateful to my former congregation for the encouragement I received during that series of studies, and am particularly indebted to Mrs Ishbel Mackay, who transcribed the sermons into a form that became the basis of this book. I am also grateful to my friends and colleagues Malcolm Maclean and Derek Thomas for their kind and enthusiastic commendations.

Once again, I wish to thank my colleagues at Day One Christian Ministries for their willingness to publish this material. My prayer is that it will become not only a means of opening up the treasures of the twenty-third Psalm, but also a blessing, both to those who already follow the Shepherd and to those who, as yet, do not.

Once again, I wish to thank my wife and family for the blessing they have been in my life. With them, the Shepherd has taken me to verdant pastures.

Iain D. Campbell

March 2009

Knowing
the Shepherd
personally

The Lord is my shepherd; I shall not want.

(v. 1)

I don't suppose there is a passage of Scripture with which people are more familiar than Psalm 23. The words of the metrical version are among the best loved and most often sung of the Scottish Metrical Psalms. Every statement of the psalm is loaded with meaning and significance. We need to spend some time walking through it.

The heading of the psalm tells us that it is a composition of David: it is a shepherd psalm written by a shepherd. David had received a great deal of his personal training in the wilderness looking after his father's sheep.

When Samuel called at Jesse's house in Bethlehem, looking to anoint one of his sons as king, David was absent, having remained loyal to his post, looking after his sheep (1 Sam. 16:11–13). God's purpose in David's life was to make him a different kind of shepherd.

It is interesting to note how the Old Testament refers to David's role as king of Israel as the 'shepherd' of Israel. The historical record tells us that the tribes came to David in Hebron and said, 'Behold, we are your bone and flesh. In times past, when Saul was king over us, it was you who led out and brought in Israel. And the Lord said to you, "You shall be shepherd of my people Israel, and you shall be prince over Israel"' (2 Sam. 5:1–2). The reason why the tribes anointed

David as king was because God had said to David, 'you will be the shepherd'. Psalm 78 expresses this beautifully:

> He chose David his servant
>> and took him from the sheepfolds;
> from following the nursing ewes he brought him
>> to shepherd Jacob his people,
>> Israel his inheritance.
> With upright heart he shepherded them
>> and guided them with his skilful hand.
>
> (Ps. 78:70–72)

Here is twofold shepherding: God took David from shepherding the sheep to be a shepherd of the people. God trained David, while he was a shepherd of sheep, to be a pastor of men.

In Psalm 23, David confesses his own need of a shepherd. However skilful he was, and however trained in exercising his pastoral office as king, it was his greatest strength to know that God was his own Shepherd.

Of course, he was not alone in making that confession. The picture of God as Shepherd runs through the Bible. When Jacob came to bless the two sons of Joseph, Ephraim and Manasseh, at the end of his life in Egypt, he used these words: 'The God before whom my fathers Abraham and Isaac walked, the God who has been my shepherd all my life long to this day, the angel who has redeemed me from all evil, bless the boys ...' (Gen. 48:15–16). Isn't that magnificent? Here is Jacob wanting a blessing for his grandsons, and the blessing he pronounces is the blessing of the God who has been his Shepherd.

Similarly, the psalmist Asaph uses this designation of God in Psalm 80:1: 'Give ear, O Shepherd of Israel, you who lead Joseph like a flock! You who are enthroned upon the cherubim, shine forth.' The psalm of praise is lifted up to the Shepherd of Israel.

The prophets, time and again, echo the same theme. Isaiah describes the Lord, the everlasting God whom he has seen in the temple, emphasizing his eternality and unchangeableness; yet he also reminds us of the tender care God has for his people: 'He will tend his flock like a shepherd; he will gather the lambs in his arms; he will carry them in his bosom, and gently lead those that are with young' (Isa. 40:11).

Similarly, Ezekiel, the prophet of visions, records the words of God as follows:

> I myself will be the shepherd of my sheep, and I myself will make them lie down, declares the Lord God. I will seek the lost, and I will bring back the strayed, and I will bind up the injured, and I will strengthen the weak, and the fat and the strong I will destroy. I will feed them in justice.
>
> (Ezek. 34:15–16)

God pledges himself to be the Shepherd of his people. When David, therefore, says, 'The Lord is my shepherd', he is highlighting one of the great and rich metaphors of the Bible.

However, it is really only through the lens of the New Testament that we can truly appreciate what is being said in this verse. We are reminded in John 10 that there is one Person who uniquely fulfils and exercises the responsibilities of a Shepherd to his people: Jesus Christ, who says, 'I am the good shepherd.'

This is who Jesus is: the one who is praised both in the psalms and in the Gospels as the Shepherd of his people. And, by making the claim 'I am the good shepherd', Jesus was deliberately and self-consciously identifying himself with the Shepherd of Israel: Jehovah (Ps. 80:1). For him to call himself the 'shepherd' was nothing less than to claim identity with Jehovah and divinity for himself.

Jesus is the Shepherd we need. Linking back to the Old Testament, with its emphasis on God the Lord as the Shepherd of the covenant people, Jesus was claiming to be that God. It is in him that we get to the heart of this image; he was the metaphor made flesh. The Bible says several things about Jesus in this connection.

Jesus is God's Shepherd

We can claim Jesus as our own only because he was first set apart to be God's unique Shepherd. David could say, 'The Lord—the one God of Israel—is my Shepherd.' But that same God is brought before us as a Trinity: Father, Son and Holy Spirit, expressly differentiated in the New Testament. And within the Trinity, God the Father can say, 'The Lord Jesus is my Shepherd.'

In what sense can he say this? He can say it as the one who set Jesus apart in the plan of salvation and covenant of redemption to be the King and Shepherd of his people. In this sense, the shepherd concept becomes more than a metaphor and an image—it becomes a messianic title applying only to the one who will redeem and save sinners.

That is how God can speak as he does in Zechariah 13: '"Awake, O sword, against my shepherd, against the man who stands next to me," declares the Lord of hosts. "Strike the shepherd, and the sheep will be scattered; I will turn my hand against the little ones ..."' (Zech. 13:7). These words were fulfilled in Jesus, as we are reminded in Matthew 26:31: 'Then Jesus said to them, "You will all fall away because of me this night. For it is written, 'I will strike the shepherd, and the sheep of the flock will be scattered ...'"' God set apart Jesus as the one who would save his people.

The messianic nature of the title is also seen in Ezekiel 34, where God promises to set a Shepherd over his people: 'I will set up over them one shepherd, my servant David, and he shall feed them: he shall feed them and be their shepherd' (Ezek. 34:23). Although David had been dead many years at this point, Ezekiel spoke of him as one still to come; ultimately, in the person and work of Jesus Christ, who described himself both as the root and the descendant of David (Rev. 22:16), this prophecy was fulfilled. Jesus is the one of whom God can say, 'He is *my* Shepherd.'

Jesus is the good Shepherd

Jesus also describes himself in John 10:11 as 'the good shepherd'. There are other shepherds, but there is none as good as this, because this Shepherd lays down his life for the sheep. That is where you find the evidence of the goodness of this particular Shepherd. The sheep have gone astray and have been disobedient, yet they are the object of his love and care to the extent that, as the good Shepherd, he is going to lay down his life for them.

This has to be combined with another image: as the one who lays down his life, this Shepherd is also the 'Lamb of God' (John 1:29), who will go silently before its shearers to save the sheep who have gone astray (Isa. 53:6–7). The badness of the sheep is contrasted with the goodness of the Shepherd/Lamb, who remains obedient to God and shows his love both for God and his people by being sacrificed on their behalf.

Jesus is the great Shepherd

Jesus is also the great Shepherd. That is made clear in the great benediction of Hebrews 13:20–21: 'Now may the God of peace who brought again from the dead our Lord Jesus, the great shepherd of the sheep, by the blood of the eternal covenant, equip you with everything good that you may do his will, working in us that which is pleasing in his sight, through Jesus Christ, to whom be glory for ever and ever.'

The good Shepherd died for his sheep; and God brought again from the dead the great Shepherd of the sheep. So we see the Lord Jesus Christ's goodness in the fact that he went to the cross, and his greatness in the fact that he was raised from the dead. At the very heart of the Christian faith stands a cross on which the good Shepherd died, and an empty grave from which the great Shepherd rose again.

Jesus is the chief Shepherd

Peter describes Jesus as 'the chief Shepherd' (1 Peter 5:4). It is very interesting that, as Peter addressed the elders of the church, he described them as shepherds. Peter himself was a shepherd—a pastor. The word 'pastor' is the Latin word for 'shepherd'; we use it to describe elders who have the care of the church and a pastoral—shepherding—role to fulfil. Peter had such a role over Christ's flock. Jesus had said to him 'Feed my sheep' and 'Feed my lambs' (John 21:15–17), and now Peter exhorted those who were elders in the church to be diligent in their calling and faithful in their pastoral ministry.

One of the motivations for such faithfulness is here: 'And when the chief Shepherd appears, you will receive the unfading crown of glory' (1 Peter 5:4). Those of us who are in authority in the church are only under the greater authority of the 'chief Shepherd'. The responsibility for the church is his; it is he who is in charge here and is the ultimate pastor of the church. The authority of every other pastor and elder is delegated.

As shepherds over the flock, elders are to look after the church as those who themselves are under the charge and care of the chief Shepherd; that chief Shepherd is going to come again and he will give a crown to his people. We may be shepherds, but none of us is chief shepherd.

Jesus is the royal Shepherd

In Revelation, John reminds us that Jesus is a royal, enthroned Shepherd. In the great vision of Revelation 7, John saw a multitude that no one could number gathered around the throne of God, which was occupied by a lamb. Of that lamb the book of Revelation says, 'For the Lamb in the midst of the throne will be their shepherd, and he will guide them to springs of living water, and God will wipe away every tear from their eyes' (Rev. 7:17).

So, in heaven, Christ, the Lamb enthroned, will have a pastoral function in relation to his church as he shepherds his people to living fountains of waters and wipes away all tears from their eyes. Here is a magnificent combination of roles and designations: the Lamb is the Shepherd of heaven, enthroned in splendour, where every eye is on him and every ear listens to him as he shepherds his people. He leads them along ever-increasing lines of praise and adoration and ever-deepening levels of understanding and knowledge. He excites them, feeding and filling them continuously; and eternity will not exhaust what this Shepherd is going to do for his flock in glory.

The Shepherd and the flock belong to each other

Psalm 23 turns on the personal pronoun 'my'—'The Lord is *my* shepherd'. David can lay personal claim to the Shepherd. The possessive is so very important—it is emphasized in this psalm. See for yourself how many times David refers to himself in the psalm. Yet it is not a psalm about him but about his Shepherd-King, his Saviour. It is a psalm about his God, and yet his own personal interests are so caught up in the glories of this relationship between his Saviour and himself that, again and again, he refers to it.

So David says of the Lord that he is 'my shepherd'. And here is the all-important question for us all: Is Jesus mine? It is one thing for me to know that he is a great and a good Shepherd, but it is something else to claim that he is mine. It is one thing to know that he fulfils all of these saving roles and functions for his people, but it is quite another to say, 'He is all of this for me.'

This is the starting point of the psalm. There is one flock and one Shepherd, and they belong to each other. The flock does not belong to anyone else, and neither does the Shepherd. The relationship is mutually exclusive. We will look at the characteristics of the flock in Chapter 7, but for now we must note the glory of the possession. A husband looks at a photograph of his wife in a way in which he cannot look at the photograph of any other woman in the world. The woman whose image he sees there—and only she—is his. Similarly, those who believe in Christ and trust in him for salvation are able to look at Jesus and say, 'He is mine.'

The consequence of having a Shepherd

If Jesus is our Shepherd, there is a very important consequence: 'I shall not want.' Psalm 34:9–10 expresses the same truth this way: '... those who fear [the Lord] have no lack! The young lions suffer want and hunger; but those who seek the Lord lack no good thing.'

In other words, if I can truly say that the Lord is my Shepherd, I will know no lack and no want in my life. Now, it is true that there may be many things missing from my life that

I could wish to be in it. There may be many issues that I need to address; but in the most fundamental sense, if Jesus and I belong to each other, I lack nothing.

Firstly, I lack nothing as far as my *soul's salvation* is concerned. Everything essential to the welfare of my soul is provided for me in the Lord Jesus Christ. That was denied in many parts of the New Testament world and the gospel was under attack at this very point, with the teaching that people needed more than Christ in order to be sure of their salvation. The apostle Paul countered this in several places in the New Testament, such as in Colossians 2:9, where he said of Jesus that 'in him the whole fullness of deity dwells bodily, and you have been filled in him'. That is the essential thing: there is a completeness, a filling, that belongs to those who are united to Christ. No supplement is required.

Secondly, if Christ is my Shepherd, I lack nothing as far as my *life situation* is concerned. My life is taken care of! In Christ's hands I have the guarantee that everything in my life is for a specific purpose. Jesus taught us in the Sermon on the Mount that the Gentiles—those outside the covenant community of the redeemed—worry about things to do with their lives: about what to eat, drink and wear (Matt. 6:25–33). But Christ turned to his disciples and said, 'Do not be anxious about any of these things.' He provides everything that his flock needs.

More than that, even the things that are unpleasant and difficult to cope with are under his care and control. He co-ordinates even the dark and difficult events so that they form part of the tapestry of my experience, all for his glory and my good. He gives more grace, and, as the psalm goes on to describe, he maintains and sustains me each step of the journey.

But there is more. Ultimately, if Jesus is my Shepherd, I lack nothing for my *ultimate destination*. That is the point around which the psalm is framed; if the Lord is my Shepherd now, I have a hope that lasts 'for ever'. He leads his flock out in order to bring it home.

It was in this way that the psalmist elsewhere described the journey of Israel from Egypt to Canaan:

> Then he led out his people like sheep
>   and guided them in the wilderness like a flock.
> He led them in safety, so that they were not afraid,
>   but the sea overwhelmed their enemies.
> And he brought them to his holy land,
>   to the mountain which his right hand had won.
> He drove out nations before them;
>   he apportioned them for a possession
>   and settled the tribes of Israel in their tents.
>
> (Ps. 78:52–55)

God shepherded his people all the way to their destination. If we are in his flock, that will be our life story, too. He may take us down roads we never expected to travel or would never have chosen for ourselves. He may take us to roads 'less travelled by', as the poet Robert Frost put it,[1] which will make all the difference to our lives. We may end up in green pastures or dark valleys, amid enemies and all alone, but the destination is always in sight. And we will lack nothing until he brings us home at last.

This thought is beautifully expressed in Henry Baker's rendering of this psalm:

> The King of love my Shepherd is,
> Whose goodness faileth never,
> I nothing lack if I am his
> And he is mine forever ...
>
> And so through all the length of days
> Thy goodness faileth never;
> Good Shepherd, may I sing thy praise
> Within thy house forever.

Reflect on these points

1. *There are other shepherds, but there is none as good as this. The sheep have gone astray and been disobedient, yet they are the object of his love and care to the extent that, as the good Shepherd, he is going to lay down his life for them.*

2. *The Lamb is the Shepherd of heaven, enthroned in splendour. He leads his sheep along ever-increasing lines of praise and adoration and ever-deepening levels of understanding and knowledge. He excites them, feeding and filling them continuously; eternity will not exhaust what this Shepherd is going to do for his flock in glory.*

3. *Here is the all-important question: Is Jesus mine? It is*

one thing for me to know that he is a great and a good Shepherd, but it is something else to claim that he is mine and to say, 'He is all of this for me.'

4. *If I can truly say that the Lord is my Shepherd, I will know no lack and no want in my life. In the most fundamental sense, if Jesus and I belong to each other, I lack nothing.*

Following the Shepherd's direction

He makes me lie down in green pastures.
He leads me beside still waters.

(v. 2)

In the opening statement of Psalm 23, David acknowledged what God was for him: that the Lord was his Shepherd. Every believer is able to make this psalm his or her own, and to make this great confession of faith: that the Lord Jesus Christ is our Shepherd.

But as we come to verse 2, we notice a subtle change. Now David is not just talking about what God *is* for him, but about what God *does* for him. The statement of faith becomes a statement of fact and moves into a description of God's work in David's life and experience. As he begins to talk about what God does for him, he says, 'My shepherd makes me lie down in green pastures and he leads me beside still waters.'

For David, the shepherd-king and author of this psalm, being a believer does not simply involve a theoretical notion about God and God's existence and character. He does believe certain things about God's being and character—no one can be a Christian without believing things about God—but for David, the essence of his life as a believer is that God is a living God to him. God's work in his life is a real and a personal thing. For David, it is not just a case of knowing about God, but knowing God through his experience. God is a reality to him as the God who is outside his life and yet is intimately involved in it.

This is fundamentally important. The psalms force us to ask whether the God whose praises are sung in them is actually in our lives and working in our lives. Is God for us merely some kind of theory or belief—or is he a living experience? Do we know the power and reality of this faith? Do we know what it is to be led by him and to know him personally?

What we are really asking is: What does it mean to be a Christian? We can try to answer that question in seven ways on the basis of the second verse of this great psalm. Being a Christian means ...

Our lives yield to one person

Being a Christian means that I belong to the flock of just one Shepherd. It is such a basic point, but it is a fundamental point. David does not say, 'I lie down in green pastures; I walk beside still waters.' The emphasis is not on what David does so much as on what the Shepherd does. '*He* makes me lie down. *He* leads me.' David has the Shepherd in his thoughts; and it is of the very essence of what it means to be a believer that our lives yield to that Shepherd.

Our lives, in other words, yield to the Lord Jesus; all our interests are in him, and we have nothing but what we have in him. To live the life of a believer is to rest completely and wholly on what Jesus is and does; it is to yield completely to his hands.

Yet that can be such a difficult thing for us to do. It is not easy for proud, self-centred, sinful man to place himself into the care of another. By nature, we are self-sufficient and self-determined. We are independent—we are going to live our way, as we want and under our own direction. But being a believer means that we yield to the Shepherd.

The image of sheep going astray is often used of man in his natural, fallen, sinful condition—man without God. The prophet Isaiah says that 'All we like sheep have gone astray; we have turned every one to his own way' (Isa. 53:6). It is an image which Peter picks up in his letter, when he describes believers in this way: 'For you were straying like sheep, but have now returned to the Shepherd and Overseer of your souls' (1 Peter 2:25). Only by returning to the Shepherd can we ever find peace.

Of course, it is easier for sheep to get lost on their own than to return home on their own! This is why the Bible presents such glorious good news, speaking of a Shepherd who has gone out looking for the lost sheep: 'I myself will be the shepherd of my sheep, and I myself will make them lie down, declares the Lord GOD. I will seek the lost, and I will bring back the strayed, and I will bind up the injured, and I will strengthen the weak ...' (Ezek. 34:15–16).

The same point is made dramatically in the story of the lost sheep in Luke 15:4–6:

> What man of you, having a hundred sheep, if he has lost one of them, does not leave the ninety-nine in the open country, and go after the one that is lost, until he finds it? And when he has found it, he lays it on his shoulders, rejoicing. And when he comes home, he calls together

his friends and his neighbours, saying to them, 'Rejoice with me, for I have found my sheep that was lost.'

Jesus applied the story in this way: 'Just so, I tell you, there will be more joy in heaven over one sinner who repents than over ninety-nine righteous persons who need no repentance' (Luke 15:7).

So this is the decisive turning point of Christian experience: from being astray and far from God, we return to him, our Shepherd. We yield to him. He has sought out the sheep that were lost and we are now in him, as he is now in us.

We surrender to the leading of Christ

The emphasis of Psalm 23:2 is that the Shepherd is leading us. We have surrendered our wills to him. He has come in and taken over. We have become, as Jesus said we must become, like little children (Matt. 18:3). As children, we lose our self-sufficiency and independence and we bow to the authority of others. That is part of what it means to be a little child. Becoming a Christian means that I must become like a little child and enter into the kingdom with my will submitted to God.

So it is with sheep, who are submissive to the leading and guiding of the shepherd. Sometimes that is not easy. Sheep need to be brought in line; the shepherd needs to use his dogs or some other means to bring the flock together to submit to his will. But here David is absolutely submitting to his Shepherd so that, where the Shepherd leads, he follows. Where the Shepherd makes him lie down, he lies down. And his life is not self-determined, but is determined by the will of the Shepherd.

We have a varied life

What David says here is so beautiful: 'Sometimes, the Shepherd brings me to green pastures. Other times, he brings me to still waters, and he is leading me along different roads and different paths, bringing me into different experiences.' In them all, David discovers many different blessings, as the Shepherd takes him to one place today and another place tomorrow. The Shepherd is guiding his life in all the variety of circumstances and blessings.

The unbeliever cannot say that. The non-Christian is not submissive to Christ and his leading and consequently has a dull life. His or her life is just being carried along by the stream of the fashions of this fallen world. If you are not born again, you are being carried along by the flow of the world's changing ideas and philosophies. Ultimately, that stream will flow all the way into a lost eternity—unless you find Jesus Christ.

But, if you do find Jesus Christ, he will fill your life with blessings beyond number, and life will never be the same again. It will never be dull again. Sometimes Jesus will take you to green pastures; sometimes he will take you beside still waters; in it all, your life will be so full of variety and blessing that you will praise him for all the different things that God has poured into it.

There is, of course, a subtle difference between the two statements of our verse. One statement speaks about stillness and restfulness—'He makes me lie down'—and the other speaks of movement and about being led and walking—'He leads me beside still waters'. So the Shepherd sometimes makes me lie down and sometimes makes me walk. Sometimes—often, perhaps—there are points in my life when he brings me to a place of stillness, while at other times my life is characterized by movement. Even within circumstances, things change; there can be a variety of stillness, with times of contemplation and of rest, while at other times God leads me on.

In other words, God provides moments when I can rest; times when, in the words of the psalmist, 'In peace I will both lie down and sleep; for you alone, O LORD, make me dwell in safety' (Ps. 4:8). Don't you just love that? Don't you love the fact that there are times in your life when there may be storms all around, but the Shepherd can give you a place of peace and security, a place of quietness and stillness in which to rest?

At other times, God rouses you, gets you moving again and takes you to other experiences. Day by day he is leading you, and life is never dull; the Word of God comes to you with such a variety of blessings and promises in such a variety of circumstances.

Solomon gives this counsel to young men about the importance of listening to the advice of their seniors:

> My son, keep your father's commandment,
>   and forsake not your mother's teaching.
> Bind them on your heart always;
>   tie them round your neck.
> When you walk, they will lead you;
>   when you lie down, they will watch over you;

and when you awake, they will talk with you.
For the commandment is a lamp and the teaching
a light ...

(Prov. 6:20–23)

The words of wise parents will lead us when we walk; and when we lie down, they will watch over us. That is what the flock of God discovers about God's Word. God leads them in different ways and makes them lie down in different paths. And all the time, his commandments will watch over us and lead us.

Blind hymnwriter Fanny Crosby put it like this:

With numberless blessings each moment he crowns;
And filled with his fullness divine,
I sing in my rapture, oh, glory to God!
For such a Redeemer as mine.[1]

It is just as Isaiah says of his heavenly Shepherd:

He will tend his flock like a shepherd;
he will gather the lambs in his arms;
he will carry them in his bosom,
and gently lead those that are with young.

(Isa. 40:11)

We have a life in which the very best conditions are created for our needs and development

As the psalm will show us, it is not always into green pastures and beside still waters that the Shepherd takes his sheep. His promise is not that we will always know tranquillity in our lives or have nice things happen to us, but that, if we belong to him, it is always the *best* things that will happen to us. They may not always be the most pleasant or the easiest things to understand, but they are always the very best conditions for us.

It is the Shepherd himself who creates these conditions for us to meet our needs at particular times. The psalm says, '*He* makes me lie down.' It is not always in our nature to lie down and rest, but sometimes he brings things into our experience and forces us to be still.

There are many things that might prevent us from lying down. Douglas MacMillan, in his book on Psalm 23, *The Lord My Shepherd*, draws on his own vast experience as a shepherd in an earlier career and says that he was always conscious that there were four things that could prevent sheep from lying down. First, *fear*—the sheep can't lie down if the dog comes and starts barking, or strangers come and start shouting. Second, *antagonism*. He describes the bully sheep, the sheep that wants to be number one in the flock and antagonizes the rest. Unless the shepherd does something drastic to keep the bully sheep from annoying the rest, the other sheep will not lie down. Third, *irritation*. Flies and insects annoy sheep and keep them moving; the sheep can't lie down if they are irritated. Fourth, *hunger*. If you see sheep lying down, they are satisfied, unafraid, not annoyed by anything and there is no antagonism; and it takes a good shepherd to create the right conditions that will allow the sheep to lie down.[2]

So it is with us. There are many things that make us afraid and antagonize us. It can take just one wrong word, said by someone out of turn, to bring all kinds of thoughts into our minds and make us restless; then our stillness is gone. But here is a Shepherd who can deal with all of these things. He can deal with the things that make us afraid. He can put all the bully sheep into perspective for us. He can deal with all the insects and all the things that annoy his sheep. He can so fill the hungry soul that he can make his sheep lie down.

When I used to help my grandfather with his sheep, I could never make the sheep lie down. I would come along and the sheep would be up and running away; but a true shepherd can do it. A shepherd can create the conditions that will enable his sheep to rest. So the Shepherd makes me lie down. Sometimes, I don't think I need to lie down, but he makes me rest. Maybe there are things that he has brought into our lives that have forced us into times of stillness and quietness. He took away from us the opportunity to be out and about as normal, and afterwards we realized that he was creating the very best life for us. Who would not want to be led by such a Shepherd as this?

We have a life in which we are constantly being nourished

This is really what the verse is saying: the Shepherd is nourishing his sheep. He is not simply leading them; he is also feeding them. He makes them lie down because they are satisfied in him Their souls never go hungry. In this sense, verse 2 is an explanation of verse 1. If the Lord is my Shepherd, I shall not be in want. When I need green pastures, he feeds me there; when I need still waters, he takes me and nourishes me there.

Do you know this in your own Christian life? Perhaps there have been times when you have felt like slowing down; you wondered if it was all getting too much for you—and then God spoke to you. Maybe a verse that you read in the Bible in your daily readings; maybe something a preacher said from the pulpit; maybe something written on a card that someone sent you; maybe a verse that you just saw somewhere—whatever it was, the Word of God came to you and you knew that this was your Lord nourishing and strengthening you.

So being a Christian means, in the words of another psalm, that 'The young lions suffer want and hunger; but those who seek the LORD lack no good thing' (Ps. 34:10).

We are guaranteed absolute security in all our circumstances

There is a beautiful picture given us here of sheep in green pastures and beside still waters. But the beautiful pastoral image hides the fact that all around there are enemies just waiting to attack the flock. As Jesus says in John 10, there are thieves and robbers—people that have absolutely no interest in the good of the Shepherd or his flock. But David just says, 'He makes me lie down.' In other words, the Shepherd worries about the security of his flock so that the flock doesn't have to.

All that the sheep see are these cool refreshing streams along which the Shepherd is taking them. They are not conscious of how the Shepherd's eye is roving all over the landscape, looking in every direction, just in case there might be some wild beast wanting to destroy the flock. The flock just lies down and leaves the worrying to the Shepherd. This is the ultimate guarantee of John 10:28: '... they will never perish, and no one will snatch them out of my hand.' So, if someone comes to this good Shepherd and points to the sheep lying down in green pastures and says, 'Look at these sheep; look at the danger they're in!', the good Shepherd just says, 'They will never perish.' There is rest and refreshment here for the sheep only because there is safety here that they cannot find anywhere else.

We live a life of progress

John Bunyan wrote a book entitled *The Pilgrim's Progress.* That was a good title: becoming a Christian is not the end of the matter but just the beginning. Knowing that the Lord is your Shepherd is just the beginning of a life of progress under his leading and care. This Shepherd has a destination in view for his flock. His ultimate intention and desire is to take his sheep home. But John tells us in the book of Revelation that, even when the sheep get home to heaven, the Lamb in the midst of the throne will be the Shepherd of his people there too, leading and shepherding them to living fountains of waters.

He is not going to make them lie down in heaven in green pastures but is going to lead them to living fountains of waters. The progress that begins here will continue in heaven and throughout eternity. The Shepherd will keep leading, and the flock will discover more and more of the blessings that he covenanted to them. That is why Proverbs can describe the life of the believer in this way: '... the path of the righteous is like the light of dawn, which shines brighter and brighter until full day' (Prov. 4:18).

Joseph Gilmore, an American preacher, recorded the following incident:

> As a young man who had recently been graduated from Brown University and Newton Theological Institution, I was supplying for a couple of Sundays the pulpit of the First Baptist Church in Philadelphia, Pennsylvania. At the midweek service on 26 March, 1862, I set out to give the people an exposition of the 23rd Psalm which I had given before on three or four occasions but, this time, I did not get further than the words 'He leadeth me.' Those words took hold of me as they had never done before and I saw in them a significance and wondrous beauty of which I had never dreamed ... It was the darkest hour of the Civil War. I did not refer to that fact but it may, subconsciously, have led me to realize that God's leadership is the one significant fact in human experience; that it makes no difference how we are led or where we are led, as long as we are sure that it is God who is leading us.

As a result, Gilmore penned these famous lines:

> He leadeth me, O blessèd thought!
> O words with heavenly comfort fraught!
> Whate'er I do, where'er I be
> Still, 'tis God's hand that leadeth me.

He leadeth me, he leadeth me
By his own hand he leadeth me;
His faithful follower I would be,
For by his hand, he leadeth me.

Sometimes midst scenes of deepest gloom,
Sometimes where Eden's flowers bloom,
By waters still, o'er troubled sea,
Still 'tis his hand that leadeth me.

So, if God is leading, are we following? If this is what the Shepherd does for his sheep and with his sheep—giving them green pastures, leading them beside still waters—are we following him?

Reflect on these points

1. *Is God for us merely some kind of theory or belief—or is he a living experience? Do we know what it is to be led by him and to know him personally?*

2. *To live the life of a believer is to rest completely and wholly on what Jesus is and does; it is to yield completely to his hands. Yet it is not easy for proud, self-centred, sinful man to place himself into the care of another.*

3. *God's promise is not that we will always know tranquillity in our lives or have nice things happen to us, but that, if we belong to him, it is always the best things that will happen to us. They may not always be the most*

pleasant or the easiest things to understand, but they are always the very best conditions for us.

4. *Knowing that the Lord is your Shepherd is just the beginning of a life of progress under his leading and care. This Shepherd has a destination in view for his flock: to take his sheep home. But even when the sheep get home to heaven, the Lamb will be the Shepherd of his people there too, leading and shepherding them to living fountains of waters.*

Experiencing
the Shepherd's
leading

He restores my soul. He leads me in paths of righteousness for his name's sake.

(v. 3)

As we have already noted, the God who is portrayed as the Shepherd of his people in this psalm is to be identified with the Lord Jesus Christ. As we work through the psalm, we not only study it in its own Old Testament context, but we also Christologize it: we read it in the light of the coming, death and resurrection of Jesus Christ.

In the first verse, as we have seen, David described what God was for him: his Shepherd. Then, in verse 2, he told us what his Shepherd did for him: he made him lie down in green pastures and led him beside still waters. Verse 3 develops that thought further: here David tells us *how* God leads him beside still waters and through green pastures. As David reflects on the pastoral care that God has over him, he is conscious of several things happening in his life; for example, that his soul, or perhaps his life, is being restored and revived, and that his strength is being renewed as the Shepherd leads him.

He is also aware of the fact that the Shepherd is leading him along certain, well-defined paths. The life of the believer is a life of variety, as we have seen. It is green pastures one moment and still waters the next. But these different avenues and paths have all got something in common. They are, to use the words of verse 3, paths of righteousness. And the psalmist comes increasingly to realize that behind everything the Shepherd does in leading him along these paths of righteousness is the Shepherd's zeal for the glory of his own name.

I think that Psalm 23 reflects the maturing of the Christian life. Here is a man who has discovered that God is a Shepherd for him and that the best possible life he can live is that lived under the direction and leading of the Shepherd. But as he goes on and matures in his faith, he comes to realize these three great things: the effect of all of this on his soul, the paths of righteousness that are common to all the ways by which the Shepherd leads, and the fact that it is zeal for his own name that is driving the Shepherd's directing of him. He comes to appreciate *how* the Shepherd leads him, *where* the Shepherd leads him, and *why* the Shepherd leads him.

How does the Shepherd lead his flock?

The Shepherd leads his flock in such a way that he himself provides the strength for the journey. That is, in essence, what the first phrase in verse 3 is teaching us. The Shepherd never leads his flock where his own grace does not restore and revive their very souls. Sometimes, the ways can be difficult and we can wander from them; at other times, we can be loaded down with burdens of one kind or another; and yet, as the Shepherd leads, he is constantly renewing our vigour and giving us encouragement—restoring our souls.

To use the language of Eugene Peterson's paraphrase of this psalm in *The Message*, God allows us 'to catch our breath'. He fills us with enough strength to go on to the next part of the journey. There he gives us enough encouragement to enable us to follow him wherever he takes us next. The more we go on, the more we realize that we could never have made it by ourselves unless the Shepherd had been constantly restoring our souls. He has been reviving our flagging spirits and putting strength and vigour into our steps, allowing us, here and there along the way, just to catch our breath.

Do you remember how God did that for Jacob? Jacob was one of the first people in the Bible to call God his Shepherd (Gen. 48:15). Jacob was led along very difficult paths, so much so that, at one point in his life, he simply said to his sons, 'You have bereaved me of my children: Joseph is no more, and Simeon is no more, and now you would take Benjamin. All this has come against me' (Gen. 42:36).

'Everything is against me.' Have you ever spoken like that? Have you ever thought that nothing was going right? Jacob thought that the events in his life were conspiring against him. He thought Joseph was dead, and there was now a threat over Benjamin. The whole family was in jeopardy.

And so it was—until a point came when Joseph, who had been testing his brothers, revealed his true identity and sent a message to his father through them:

> And they told him, 'Joseph is still alive, and he is ruler over all the land of Egypt.' And his heart became numb, for he did not believe them. But when they told him all the words of Joseph, which he had said to them, and when he saw the wagons that Joseph

had sent to carry him, the spirit of their father Jacob
revived.

(Gen. 45:26–27)

Joseph sent chariots and provisions to his father. It was all the
proof Jacob needed that Joseph was still alive.

Don't you love that? 'The spirit of their father Jacob
revived.' It had been flagging and despondent, but now there
was reason to hope and to carry on. The crushing weight that
had been on him was suddenly released as he was presented
with evidence that Joseph was now governor in the land of
Egypt. God restored his soul and made him buoyant again.
He caught his breath and was ready to take the next step of his
pilgrimage, all the way into Egypt.

Something similar happens in the book of Ruth, one of my
favourite books in the Bible. Sometimes I wonder if it should
be called the book of Naomi. Naomi, Ruth's mother-in-law,
is one of the main characters of the book. At the beginning of
the story, she follows her husband into Moab, thinking that
Moab will supply what the land of Judah lacks. Instead, Moab
takes everything from her, and Naomi ends up weeping over
the graves of her sons and her husband. Her testimony is, 'I
went away full, and the LORD has brought me back empty.
Why call me Naomi [which means "pleasant"], when the LORD
has testified against me and the Almighty has brought calamity
upon me?' (Ruth 1:21). In Ruth 1, Naomi has this crushing
weight of pain on her spirits; but when we see her in chapter
4, nursing the son of Ruth and cradling him in her arms, all

the women of the village sing, 'Blessed be the LORD, who has not left you this day without a redeemer, and may his name be renowned in Israel! He shall be to you a restorer of life ...' (4:14–15). This is what God did for her: he restored her soul. He gave her new strength and vigour, like a good shepherd encouraging his flock.

Augustine translates this phrase in Psalm 23:3 as 'He will convert my soul'. We use the word 'convert' to refer to the initial change that takes place in a person's life when he or she is born again. But when Christ predicted Peter's denial and gave him a promise of restoration, he said to him, '... when you have turned again, strengthen your brothers' (Luke 22:32). 'When you are converted ...' Peter needed to be converted all over again. That is how it is with us: we need to be born again once, but converted often.

Maybe you have experienced that; at points along the way you've given in to doubt and despair, despondency and darkness, and you have wondered if you were ever born again at all. Then God comes to you and restores your soul, and you are converted all over again. He sets you on your way. That is why Paul can say, 'we do not lose heart' (2 Cor. 4:1). The way may be difficult but we don't lose heart. The outward man is perishing, but the inward man is being renewed and restored (2 Cor. 4:16). That is how God leads his people.

Where does the Shepherd lead his flock?

The Shepherd leads his people to different situations and circumstances. No two believers are walking the same road, and the road that we are walking today may not be the road that we will walk tomorrow. Psalm 23 talks of still waters, green pastures and the valley of the shadow of death. But these paths are all 'paths of righteousness'.

This is a very interesting phrase. The word 'righteousness' is a very important one in the Bible. Almost a quarter of its uses in the Old Testament come in the book of Psalms. Sometimes it is used of God, sometimes of the believer and sometimes, as here, simply about what is right. Paths of righteousness are right paths, just as in Psalm 4:5 'sacrifices of righteousness' (KJV) are 'right sacrifices' (ESV).

God leads his people along right paths. They may be very different paths, but they are all right paths. Left to themselves, the sheep would wander onto paths of sin, and these would be wrong paths. Shepherds need to guide their sheep in the right way; by themselves, that is not where the flock will go. Psalm 119:176 says, 'I have gone astray like a lost sheep; seek your servant, for I do not forget your commandments.' There it is: the right path is the path of the commandments, the path of righteousness. But what are paths of righteousness?

Paths of righteousness are, first of all, paths that accord with the perfect will of God. The Shepherd leads his people according to his will. In this flock, the sheep are content to let the Shepherd do the leading because they know that his will for them is the best possible thing that could govern their lives. Our present situation may be very difficult, but if our trust is in the Shepherd and we are walking in his will, then our situation is the best possible situation for us. It is a path of righteousness; it accords perfectly with his will for us. Perhaps it will take until we get to heaven for us to realize that the paths that we thought were most wrong for us were, in actual fact, most right. Maybe the Shepherd is whispering to us, as he whispered to a member of his flock long ago, 'What I am doing you do not understand now, but afterwards you will understand' (John 13:7). But we know that his will is best.

Secondly, paths of righteousness not only accord with the perfect will of God, but they also accord with the perfect Word of God. That is why, time and time again, the book of Psalms reflects on life as a pilgrimage and a pathway that can best be directed by God's Word and law. For example, here is the psalmist's 'credo' in Psalm 119:59–64:

> When I think on my ways,
>   I turn my feet to your testimonies;
> I hasten and do not delay
>   to keep your commandments.
> Though the cords of the wicked ensnare me,
>   I do not forget your law.
> At midnight I rise to praise you,
>   because of your righteous rules.
> I am a companion of all who fear you,
>   of those who keep your precepts.
> The earth, O LORD, is full of your steadfast love;
>   teach me your statutes!

Psalm 119 is really the psalm of an individual sheep. But if we want to walk according to the leading of the Shepherd, we need to pay attention to what the rest of the flock are doing. If we value our lives and walk in the right way, then, like the psalmist, we will covet the path of God's commandments, and we will discover them by reading his Word and studying it in the company of others. The best way to avoid the paths of sin is to walk the paths of righteousness, and the best way to walk these is to have as much exposure to the claims of God's Word as we possibly can.

Thirdly, paths of righteousness are paths that accord with the Shepherd's own example. In the last chapter we quoted from 1 Peter 2, where Peter says that, instead of continuing to go astray, we have returned to the Shepherd of our souls. But what is the context of that verse? It is this: 'Christ also suffered for you, leaving you an example, so that you might follow in his steps' (1 Peter 2:21). He was the Lamb of God, and his life was one of righteousness. The life of the Christian is the life of the Christlike one. God's purpose with us is to make us as much like Jesus as possible, and this begins here and now.

To what end does the Shepherd lead his flock?

He does it for the sake of his name, or, as one metrical rendering puts it, 'This he has done his great name to display.' This point was made by Ezekiel too, as God spoke about the work he had done for his people:

> I acted for the sake of my name, that it should not be
> profaned in the sight of the nations among whom they

lived, in whose sight I made myself known to them in bringing them out of the land of Egypt. So I led them out of the land of Egypt and brought them into the wilderness. I gave them my statutes and made known to them my rules, by which, if a person does them, he shall live. Moreover, I gave them my Sabbaths, as a sign between me and them, that they might know that I am the LORD who sanctifies them. But the house of Israel rebelled against me in the wilderness. They did not walk in my statutes but rejected my rules, by which, if a person does them, he shall live; and my Sabbaths they greatly profaned.

Then I said I would pour out my wrath upon them in the wilderness, to make a full end of them. But I acted for the sake of my name …

(Ezek. 20:9–14)

'I acted', God says, 'for the sake of my name.' This is what is written over the entire redemptive history of the people of God. It was all 'for his name's sake'. Why did he redeem his people out of Egypt? Was it because they deserved it? Not at all: it was for his name's sake. Why did he not judge them in the wilderness that first moment when they rebelled against him, when they fell down and worshipped the golden calf? Why did he not just open heaven, pour out his wrath upon them and let hell devour them in an instant? It was for the sake of his great name.

All that God does for his people is motivated by his zeal for the glory of his name. This is magnificent theology. God saves me for his own glory! God keeps me for his own glory! And, interestingly, the psalmist takes this theology and turns it into prayer:

> For your name's sake, O LORD,
>   pardon my guilt, for it is great.
>
>   (Ps. 25:11)

> Incline your ear to me;
>   rescue me speedily!
> Be a rock of refuge for me,
>   a strong fortress to save me!
> For you are my rock and my fortress;
>   and for your name's sake you lead me
>   and guide me ...
>
>   (Ps. 31:2–3)

Here is the basis on which a sinner with very great sin can come to a very great and holy God and ask for pardon: for the sake of his name. And for that same reason, we know that God will lead us on right paths. God's name, reputation and glory are bound up with the safety and security of his flock. Not one sheep will be lost, or else he will have to answer for it. None will perish, or else he will be forever accountable. This is what Christ so movingly expresses in John 6:38–40:

> For I have come down from heaven, not to do my own will but the will of him who sent me. And this is the will of him who sent me, that I should lose nothing of all

that he has given me, but raise it up on the last day. For this is the will of my Father, that everyone who looks on the Son and believes in him should have eternal life, and I will raise him up on the last day.

The bedrock of our salvation is not how committed we are to God, nor even how committed he is to us; it is how committed he is to himself and to his own glory. Peter denied Christ in spite of his commitment to follow him to prison and even death. He discovered, the hard way, just how shallow our commitments and promises can be. In the light of this, he describes God's people as those who

by God's power are being guarded through faith for a salvation ready to be revealed in the last time. In this you rejoice, though now for a little while, if necessary, you have been grieved by various trials, so that the tested genuineness of your faith—more precious than gold that perishes though it is tested by fire—may be found to result in praise and glory and honour at the revelation of Jesus Christ.

(1 Peter 1:5–7)

In the end, it is all about the Shepherd's reputation. He will be praised, and he will have glory and honour throughout all eternity. With that end in view, he will always take his flock on right paths and he will present them in glory, and for glory, at last.

Reflect on these points

1. *The Shepherd never leads his flock where his own grace does not restore and revive their very souls.*

2. *The more we go on, the more we realize that we could never have made it by ourselves unless the Shepherd had been constantly restoring our souls. He has been reviving our flagging spirits and putting strength into our steps, allowing us, here and there along the way, just to catch our breath.*

3. *The Shepherd leads his people to different situations and circumstances. No two believers are walking the same road, and the road that we are walking today may not be the road that we will walk tomorrow. But these paths are all 'paths of righteousness'.*

4. *All that God does for his people is motivated by his zeal for the glory of his name. God saves me for his own glory! God keeps me for his own glory! And for that reason, we know that God will lead us on right paths. God's name, reputation and glory are bound up with the safety and security of his flock.*

Enjoying the Shepherd's protection

Even though I walk through the valley of the shadow of death, I will fear no evil, for you are with me; your rod and your staff, they comfort me.

(v. 4)

This psalm is not only a king writing about a King, it is also a shepherd writing about a Shepherd. As we have already noted, this shepherding metaphor gives us great insight into the relationship between God and his people, and it is an image that God uses over and over again in the Old Testament to describe his relationship with Israel. As God's people, we have the same relationship with God that Israel had, so that, when Jesus says, 'I am the good shepherd', we can fill out the true meaning of this psalm.

David has been talking about what God is to him and what God does for him. He has reflected on things that have been to his advantage—things that have encouraged him and lifted him up. His soul has been restored as he has followed the Shepherd. But now we come to verse 4 and, all of a sudden, this psalm strikes a very different note. David still talks about walking, only it is not now by green pastures or still waters, but in a place where everything seems to be taken from him. 'Yet,' he says, 'even walking through the valley of the shadow of death, I will fear no evil.'

Before we come to look at the substance of this assurance, we need to note some subtle changes that take place here. The first is that David has moved from talking about actual things that he has experienced to things that he has not yet experienced. He has been talking about the Shepherd having taken him to green pastures and still waters. David experienced those things, and in those places he found encouragement and strength. But now he is talking about things that he might experience. He hasn't yet walked in the valley of the shadow of death, but he is saying, 'Even were I to walk there, I would fear no evil.'

Strangely, even though these things have not yet happened in his life, they still cast a long shadow over his experience. Don't we all feel that at times? There may be difficult things that we have passed through and for which the Lord has given us extraordinary grace, and yet the unknown future gives us more cause for fear than the worst thing we have experienced in the past. It is very often the case that, as we go along life's way, we look into the future and worry about things that have not yet taken place.

So David anticipates situations that are looming on his horizon. Yet, because of his confidence in the shepherding care of God, he expresses as much confidence for the future as he professed his awareness of God's presence in the past.

Being Christians means that we can do that. We can have confidence even for the things we have not yet experienced but that nonetheless cause us anxiety and dread. If God is our Shepherd in Christ, we too can say, 'I will fear no evil.' So that is the first change here: David moves from talking about things he has *actually* experienced to things that he has not experienced yet.

But, secondly, he moves from talking about pleasant things to talking about things that are not quite so pleasant. He has been reflecting on good times and places, on good moments and green pastures. There are good and pleasant things in the Christian life. But the melody that makes up the tune of the believer's life has low notes as well. The bass notes and the minor keys also play a role. There are some preachers who promise green pastures for ever, yet the Bible never makes that promise. The people of God in the Bible are sometimes driven into 'wits' end corner' and can sing psalms like this:

> You have put me in the depths of the pit,
>   in the regions dark and deep.
> Your wrath lies heavy upon me,
>   and you overwhelm me with all your waves.
> You have caused my companions to shun me;
>   you have made me a horror to them.
> I am shut in so that I cannot escape;
>   my eye grows dim through sorrow.
> Every day I call upon you, O LORD;
>   I spread out my hands to you.

> (Ps. 88:6–9)

The book of Psalms contains many songs for people who feel utterly alone and cut off from all their friends, who are in a place where it is almost as if God has forgotten them. That is the reality of our Christian experience. It is not all green pastures and still waters; there are dark valleys, too.

But, thirdly, there is something else that changes subtly

at this point. In verse 4, David moves from talking *about* the Shepherd to talking *to* the Shepherd. He moves from using the third person to using the second person. In verses 1 to 3, he has been talking about the Shepherd and what he has done: 'The LORD is my shepherd ... *He* makes me lie down in green pastures. *He* leads me beside still waters. *He* restores my soul.' But now he directly addresses God: 'Even though I walk through the valley of the shadow of death ... *you* are with me.'

It is one thing to talk *about* God, but it is something entirely different to talk *to* God. Sometimes we can say a lot about God. We can make orthodox statements and ask biblical questions. We can discuss the God of the Bible and can enjoy doing so. But it is easier sometimes to speak about God than to address him directly with our concerns and burdens.

Do you speak about this Shepherd? It is good to do that. But far better to speak *to* the Shepherd. Have you ever spoken to God the way David spoke to God? That was David's only antidote to worry and despair over this unknown future. It was not enough for him to discuss and declare the orthodox doctrine; he needed to speak to him! And this was also Paul's answer to the neuroses that arise from living in a fallen world: '... do not be anxious about anything, but in everything by prayer and supplication with thanksgiving let your requests be made known to God. And the peace of God, which surpasses all understanding, will guard your hearts and your minds in Christ Jesus' (Phil. 4:6–7).

So what is this place in which David imagines himself

walking? He calls it 'the valley of the shadow of death'. If you are familiar with John Bunyan's *Pilgrim's Progress*, you will perhaps remember that Bunyan portrays Christian as walking through two valleys. The first of them he calls 'the valley of humiliation'. It is not an easy valley. It is a valley in which Christian has to fight with his enemy, Apollyon, who represents the devil. In our Christian lives, God sometimes leads us to points of warfare with the devil.

But, as if that were not bad enough, Christian then comes to what Bunyan calls 'the valley of the shadow of death'. Bunyan says that Christian looks into the valley and thinks he should go back, but he knows that, to get to the Celestial City, he has to go through this valley. Heaven is on the other side of it. Christian realizes that it is a very narrow and dangerous road, with a ditch on one side and mire on the other. When he tries to avoid the ditch, he nearly falls into the mire; and when he tries to avoid the mire, he nearly falls into the ditch.

He also discovers that none of the weapons that he used in the fight in the valley of humiliation are any good in this valley of the shadow of death. There is only one thing he can do: take up the weapon of *prayer*. As he prays, he thinks he can hear the voice of a man saying, 'Though I walk through the valley of the shadow of death, I will fear none ill.' From this, Christian takes courage, realizing that others of God's people have walked through this valley too; if God was with them, God will be with him.

Surely that is the message we should take from this verse. We too can listen to David, contemplating this long, lonely walk in this difficult place and saying, 'I will fear no evil, because you are with me.' If God was with David, God will be with us. Let's highlight three things here.

The name of the valley

It is called the valley of the shadow of death. It is interesting to note that David first came to prominence in a valley, where Goliath, the giant, threatened the people of God. Israel was encamped on one hill; the Philistines were encamped on another hill; and in the valley, there was a giant to face.

Here David contemplates another valley with a different giant. By definition, a valley is located between hills. There are high points in this psalm: at the beginning, where there are green pastures and still waters, quiet moments and great blessings, and at the end, when the psalmist comes into the house of the Lord. But between these two peaks runs the valley.

And it has ever been thus for God's people. There were two mountain peaks in Job's experience. At the very beginning of the book of Job, we read that 'this man [Job] was the greatest of all the people of the east' (1:3). That is some statement. Then, at the end of the book, we read that the Lord gave Job twice as much as he had before. So, if he was the greatest at the beginning, he was twice as great at the end. And yet, between these two mountain peaks, ran the valley through which he walked and said, 'I can't even begin to find God here. I look on my right hand: he is not there; on my left hand:

he is not there. I call to him, and he is not answering. Where is God?' (see Job 23).

Between moments of blessing here and glory beyond runs the valley of the shadow of death. I am sure you will have discovered that deep valleys run between mountains of blessing in the Christian life. The path to heaven is not by a cool, clear, refreshing stream all the time. Between mountain peaks of encouragement there are deep ravines to be walked.

As a shepherd in the rugged terrain of Judah, David knew the dangers of such ravines. George Adam Smith, an experienced traveller and geographer of the Holy Land, wrote that

> ... on the boundless Eastern pastures, so different from the narrow meadows and dyked hillsides with which we are familiar, the shepherd is indispensable ... I do not remember ever to have seen in the East a flock of sheep without a shepherd. In such a landscape as Judea, where a day's pasture is thinly scattered over an unfenced tract of country, covered with delusive paths, still frequented by wild beasts, and rolling off into the desert, the man and his character are indispensable.[1]

The sheep are constantly in danger in these ravines and on these paths. The shepherd's skill and care are absolutely vital.

But what causes the difficulties of the valley? Death does! David is not referring to his own death when he talks about walking 'through the valley of the shadow of death'. He is talking about experiences caused by the fact and reality of death that leave him where he is. He is thinking of the fact that dangers await his flock with every step they take. And it is no different for us. Hear is how John Calvin describes our lives:

> Innumerable are the evils that beset human life; innumerable, too, the deaths that threaten it. We need not go beyond ourselves; since our body is the receptacle of a thousand diseases—in fact holds within itself and fosters the causes of diseases—a man cannot go about unburdened by many forms of his own destruction and without drawing out a life enveloped, as it were, with death ... Your house, continually in danger of fire, threatens in the daytime to impoverish you, at night even to collapse upon you. Your field, since it is exposed to hail, frost, drought and other calamities, threatens you with barrenness and famine ... Amid these tribulations must not man be most miserable, since, but alive in life, he weakly draws his anxious and languid breath, as if he had a sword perpetually hanging over his neck?[2]

Calvin's point is not to make us morbid—in fact, in the context, he is writing to assure us that, if we trust in God's providence, we have the greatest blessing. But his point is well taken—in the midst of life, we are in death.

Sometimes death comes very close to us. Perhaps it is the death of a loved one whom you thought you would be able to hold onto much longer. Maybe your loved one was ready to go but you were not ready to let him or her go; then death came in, casting a shadow over the life and the path that you have to walk.

Maybe death has cast its shadow in other ways. Maybe some issue connected with our own health or wellbeing has suddenly made us face questions for which we have no answer. Perhaps death has come so close that it has cast its shadow over our experience and we have had to walk in that darkness for a while. The reality is that there are questions and issues that only God can answer for us, and death is one of them.

And yet there is something magnificent even here. It is not pleasant to walk under that shadow—but it is only a shadow. And that is because there is light behind it. I have only very rarely experienced a solar eclipse. The moon comes between the earth and the sun and we are plunged into an unusual and unnatural darkness. This is not our usual experience; ordinarily we stand in the light of the sun, not in the shadow of the moon. Yet there are moments of eclipse in our lives.

The light of the sun reappears when the moon continues in its orbit and the eclipse passes, but while the moon comes in-between us and the light, it is terrifying. Similarly, death comes in-between us and our happiness; it stalks us constantly, and the prospect of experiencing its effects is terrifying. Yet there is light—our Saviour 'abolished death and brought life and immortality to light through the gospel' (2 Tim. 1:10). And it is that light—the light of the resurrection of Christ—that makes death a shadow: a terrifying shadow, certainly, but nonetheless only a shadow.

The journey through the valley

So what is it like to journey through this valley? The valley of the shadow of death can be a very lonely place. The Shepherd causes all his flock to lie down by the still waters and green pastures and yet, as David contemplates the valley of the shadow, he knows, like Job and the psalmist in Psalm 88, that he has to go it alone. That itself can be hard. It is good to be part of a group. But what about when you have to go it alone? That is what David is contemplating: 'even though *I* walk ...'

Then he says, 'Even though I *walk* ...' The valley of the shadow is not a place for lying down, unlike the green pastures or the still waters; nor is it a place where you can run. It is a place where your pace is reduced to walking. Have you experienced that in your life? Have there not been moments when God has slowed you right down to walking pace? There has been no staying, resting or lying down, and no going back; but there's no running forward, either. Sometimes we would like to run, but God slows us down.

Then he reveals another aspect of the journey. David does not say, 'Even though I walk *in* the valley of the shadow of death', he talks about walking *through* the valley. There is a world of difference between walking *in* the valley and walking *through* the valley. If you are walking *through*, you know that you will come out of the valley on the other side. That is David's great confidence; however difficult and dark this valley will be for him, when the light is eclipsed and the shadow falls, when he is lonely and there is no place for him to go, he knows that it will only be temporary. One day, in God's time, he will walk out of the valley and at last leave it all behind.

That is why God's people will choose heaven anytime, and not just instead of hell. Everyone would choose heaven over hell, but God's people choose heaven over the earth itself. Even though their path to glory may be through the worst places of the earth, where they will forfeit and lose everything they have, they would rather have Christ with all of these crosses than possess the world and not have him at all. Like Moses, they choose to suffer affliction with the people of God instead of enjoying the pleasures of sin.

To get Christ with all the very worst he can give you is better than having the world and not having Christ at all. The pace may be slow and the route lonely, but walking through the valley means knowing that at last he will bring you safely out on the other side.

Peace in the valley

Finally, there is David's great assurance of peace in the valley. He has great confidence for the future. He says, 'Even though I walk through the valley of the shadow of death, I will fear no evil.' He is not saying, 'I will not fear'; there are moments when it would be quite unnatural not to be afraid. But he says, 'I will fear no evil.'

Isn't it sad that this beautiful psalm has to be spoiled by a reference to evil? But that is what has happened to God's good world. From Genesis to Revelation, we cannot escape the presence of evil. Christ died on the cross to save me 'from this present evil age' (Gal. 1:4). Evil is all around us. 'We do not wrestle', says Paul, 'against flesh and blood, but against the rulers, against the authorities, against the cosmic powers over this present darkness, against the spiritual forces of evil in the heavenly places' (Eph. 6:12).

What a privilege, therefore, for valley travellers to know that there is one who died and rose again and intercedes at God's right hand, saying to his Father for his church, 'I am not praying that you should take them out of the world, but that you should keep them from the evil one' (see John 17:15). That is what David is saying to us in the psalm; we cannot avoid the valley, or its loneliness, darkness or difficulty, but, however difficult and dark it may be, however much we may say like Job, 'Oh, that I knew where I might find him' (Job 23:3), we can also say, 'I will not be afraid of evil.'

But what is David's assurance in the valley of the shadow? First there is the reality of the Shepherd's presence with him: 'I will fear no evil, *for you are with me.*' It may be a lonely valley, but this sheep is not alone in the valley. The glory of the covenant of God's grace is that our God comes to us and says, 'Fear not, for I have redeemed you; I have called you by name, you are mine. When you pass through the waters, I will be with you' (Isa. 43:1–2). There is nothing that can guarantee our peace in the present and our assurance for the future quite like those words, 'I will be with you'. Paul knew it. He said in 2 Timothy 4:16, 'In my trial, no one stood with me.' Imagine it. You expect friends to turn up and they don't. You expect to get a letter saying, 'We're thinking of you', but no one writes one. You expect to get a text or an email that says, 'It will be all right, we are with you all the way.' But the phone and computer are silent.

So friends let Paul down. But Christ did not: 'But the Lord stood by me and strengthened me' (2 Tim. 4:17). That is the glory of being a Christian: the unfailing, abiding presence of Christ by the Holy Spirit. It is unmistakable and real: 'I am with you always, to the end of the age' (Matt. 28:20).

David was also aware of the Shepherd's *protection* of him. That is why he says, '... your rod and your staff, they comfort me.' Isn't it amazing? Walking through this lonely valley, Job said, 'I don't know where God is', but at the same time he also said, 'He knows where I am' (see Job 23:10). You see, in order to be safe, the sheep does not need to see where the Shepherd is. It is enough to know that the Shepherd knows where the sheep is: that he is with his flock and protecting his flock. His rod has the effect of guarding against every enemy that is prowling around, looking to attack the flock; and his staff is ready to keep the sheep on the right way.

These themes are woven into all the psalms in this part of the Psalter. Psalm 22 shows us Jesus the Servant, taking a cross on his shoulders. Psalm 24 shows us Jesus the Sovereign, wearing a crown on his head. But Psalm 23 shows us Jesus the Shepherd, with a crook in his hand, guiding, protecting, watching over and keeping his people even in the darkest of circumstances. The cross is past; the crown is even now on Jesus's head and is still to be displayed in its splendour. In our own lives, it is enough to know that the Shepherd's crook is in his hand and that with it he guides and protects his people.

The ESV rendering of Psalm 49:14 talks about 'Death' being the shepherd of those who do not know God. What a thought—apart from Jesus Christ, all is death and death is our shepherd. And what a contrast for those who can say in death's shadow, 'The Lord is my Shepherd', and who can contemplate even the worst of circumstances in this life and say, 'I will fear no evil, for you are with me; your rod and your staff, they comfort me.'

Robert Murray McCheyne expressed it well:

> Even treading the valley, the shadow of death,
> This watchword shall rally my faltering breath;
> And when from life's fever my God sets me free,
> Jehovah Tsidkenu my death song shall be.[3]

Nothing else comes near this to give us real peace in the valley.

Reflect on these points

1. *Being Christians means that we can have confidence even for the things we have not yet experienced but that nonetheless cause us anxiety and dread. If God is our Shepherd in Christ, we too can say, 'I will fear no evil.'*

2. *Between moments of blessing here and glory beyond runs the valley of the shadow of death. Deep valleys run between mountains of blessing in the Christian life.*

3. *However difficult and dark this valley is, when the light is eclipsed and the shadow falls, when he is lonely and*

there is no place for him to go, David knows that it will only be temporary. One day, in God's time, he will walk out of the valley and at last leave it all behind.

4. *To get Christ with all the very worst he can give you is better than having the world and not having Christ at all. The pace may be slow and the route lonely, but walking through the valley means knowing that at last he will bring you safely out on the other side.*

5. *In order to be safe, the sheep does not need to see where the Shepherd is. It is enough to know that the Shepherd knows where the sheep is.*

Trusting the Shepherd's provision

You prepare a table before me in the presence of my enemies; you anoint my head with oil; my cup overflows.

(v. 5)

We have already noted that, in the short space of this six-verse psalm, David uses the personal pronoun 'I' or 'my' over and over again. He says that 'The LORD is *my* shepherd; *I* shall not want', and so on. Here again, in verse 5, David speaks about various things that are in his life and that God has done for him, in providing for him in his journey. He continues to reflect on the goodness of the Shepherd to him and his experience of the lavish grace of God.

It is important to underscore this fact. There are some commentators who think that the metaphor keeps changing in the course of the psalm. Some suggest that, while at the beginning we have the image of a shepherd looking after his sheep, the image changes to that of a guide leading a pilgrim through the valley of the shadow of death, with the final image of a host looking after his guests. That is a very helpful way to look at the psalm, but I do think that the shepherd/sheep imagery runs right through the psalm. The whole psalm, I believe, is to be read through the lens of that initial confession, 'The LORD is my shepherd'. So it is part of God's shepherding care of us that, even in the wilderness, he prepares a table for his flock.

God's people in the wilderness asked the question, 'Can God spread a table in the wilderness?' (Ps. 78:19). God rebuked them for it. They were really asking, 'Can God supply our need in the wilderness?' Many of them doubted that it was possible and even expressed the longing to be back in Egypt, regretting that they had ever left Egypt at all (Num. 11:1–14). David had proved the point, however: even in the most difficult of circumstances, he was aware of God preparing a table for him. In a sense, Psalm 23 answers the question of Psalm 78.

Here David highlights four different things in his experience. He talks, firstly, about his enemies, secondly, about his table, thirdly, about his head, and, fourthly, about his cup. We can reflect on these in at least three different ways.

We can talk about these things as literal and powerful realities in David's own life. We can reflect on David's enemies, of which he had many—from Philistine giants to rebellious sons. We can think about how God provided for David in his life, how he anointed David's head with oil and how David's cup overflowed.

But we can apply this to Jesus, David's greater son, too. Jesus was also surrounded by enemies—he came to destroy the chief enemy of the souls of his people. Yet God anointed him and made provision for him. God gave him a cup which was a cup of suffering, yet which overflowed at last with blessing for his people.

But then we must also apply this verse to ourselves in our own Christian lives. We can think about *our* enemies, *our* table, *our* head and *our* cup. The four elements in this verse can all be applied in these three different ways.

David's enemies

David had been a shepherd once, and he knew all about how exposed his sheep were to the enemies of the flock. In the famous incident with Goliath, David explicitly referred to that very thing. 'Your servant', he said to Saul, 'used to keep sheep for his father. And when there came a lion, or a bear, and took a lamb from the flock, I went after him and struck him and delivered it out of his mouth' (1 Sam. 17:34–35). David recalled an occasion when a bear had actually snatched a lamb and he took the lamb out of the jaw of the bear. David knew all about the dangers to which a flock is exposed.

In the New Testament, that same idea is applied to the church itself. In John 10, Jesus describes himself as the good Shepherd, and part of that function is to defend the flock. Unlike the hired hand who cares more about his pay than about his sheep, a good shepherd doesn't run away when the wolf comes. A man who has just been hired to look after the flock does not protect the flock. The flock does not belong to him, and he cares more about himself than about them. But a good shepherd looks after his sheep.

Similarly, those who pastor God's flock are to protect the flock from enemies. Paul said as much to the elders of Ephesus when he spoke to them at Miletus:

> Pay careful attention to yourselves and to all the flock, of which the Holy Spirit has made you overseers, to care for the church of God, which he obtained with his own blood. I know that after my departure fierce wolves will

come in among you, not sparing the flock; and from among your own selves will arise men speaking twisted things, to draw away the disciples after them.

(Acts 20:28–30)

The flock is constantly in danger; there are enemies all around. The book of Psalms registers this danger often. The word 'enemies' appears over fifty times in the Psalter. It is used in the singular about twenty-three or so times. In his personal life, David was no stranger to being surrounded by enemies. His greatest trial came when his son became his enemy. Flattered by the praises of men, Absalom listened to the advice of Ahithophel, who was constantly looking for the weak spots in David's life, seeking a point at which he could strike him down. Ominously, the Bible says that 'the advice seemed right in the eyes of Absalom and all the elders of Israel' (2 Sam. 17:4). David knew that, as God's anointed king, he was the object of enemies all around.

It is impossible to speak of the Lord as our Shepherd without also speaking about enemies. The moment you belong to the flock of God, you will have enemies, just as surely as David had, as his flock had and as the church has had in every age and generation. If you are a Christian, the devil is your enemy. You have to be watchful. 'Your adversary the devil prowls around like a roaring lion, seeking someone to devour' (1 Peter 5:8). He is not far away from us if we belong to the flock of Jesus Christ.

The world itself can be your enemy; its godlessness,

secularism, self-interest and pleasure-seeking lifestyle are all the enemies of the flock of Jesus Christ. 'Do you not know', says James, 'that friendship with the world is enmity with God? Therefore whoever wishes to be a friend of the world makes himself an enemy of God' (James 4:4). John, one of the greatest sheep that was ever in Christ's flock, says to us, 'Do not love the world or the things in the world. If anyone loves the world, the love of the Father is not in him' (1 John 2:15). He continues, 'For all that is in the world—the desires of the flesh and the desires of the eyes and pride in possessions—is not from the Father but is from the world. And the world is passing away along with its desires, but whoever does the will of God abides for ever' (1 John 2:16–17). Around us every day, at work, in our leisure, from when we rise in the morning until we go to bed at night, the world is the enemy of all those who say, 'The Lord is my Shepherd.'

But there is something even more sobering. Our own sinful natures are our greatest enemy. 'I urge you', says Peter, 'as sojourners and exiles to abstain from the passions of the flesh, which wage war against your soul' (1 Peter 2:11). It is a sobering thought—my own sinful passions, residing in my heart, have the potential to do great damage. The choice I have to make is whether to align myself with the Shepherd, knowing that all these great powers and forces will be against me, trying to harm me; or to take the path of least resistance, living like the world and indulging in all the pleasures of sin. Like Ahithophel (2 Sam. 17:2), the devil is saying, 'I'll come upon him while he is weary'; the world is saying, 'I'll come upon him while he is discouraged'; and the flesh is saying, 'I'll throw him into a panic.' This is the conspiracy against the flock of the Shepherd-King Jesus Christ.

David's table

As our verse continues, it is in the very presence of these enemies that the Shepherd provides for his sheep. The Shepherd is only too aware that the flock is surrounded by bears and lions; as he keeps these enemies at bay, he provides for the flock. All the wild animals can do is look on as the sheep enjoy the Shepherd's provision.

We've already see in 2 Samuel 17 how Ahithophel conspired against David. He said to Absalom, 'I'll get David tonight.' But see what a fool Ahithophel is; his plans come to nothing and, at the end of the chapter, he goes out and commits suicide. He can't get David. The chapter ends with David's loyal friends coming to him and bringing provisions for David and his people who are hungry in the wilderness. So there is David, with all these enemies around him, sitting down to eat because God has provided a table for him even in the wilderness.

This is what God does for his people. Knowing that they are the objects of unrelenting attack, God's flock can become weary and discouraged. Sometimes they don't know how they are going to take another step along the way—then God comes to them and sets a table before them.

God so overrules the events of our lives that the table of his providence has good things for us to enjoy. They may not always be easy or pleasant things, but they are good. Even when God sends difficult things our way, he works them for our good. Sometimes we find ourselves in places not of our own making or choosing, but, if God is our Shepherd, we will have reason to bless him that he brought us there. Is it not the case that the things that have influenced us most are not those that we chose for ourselves but those that we did not choose? Woven into these difficulties and discouragements are good things on the table of God's providence.

Perhaps William Cowper's hymn expresses it best:

> God moves in a mysterious way
> His wonders to perform;
> He plants his footsteps in the sea,
> And rides upon the storm ...
>
> Ye fearful saints, fresh courage take;
> The clouds ye so much dread
> Are big with mercy, and shall break
> In blessings on your head ...
>
> His purposes will ripen fast,
> Unfolding every hour;
> The bud may have a bitter taste,
> But sweet will be the flower.[1]

So there are blessings to be enjoyed, even in darkness and amid discouragement. Often these good things could not have been experienced by us had God not brought us into these difficult places. Would God have prepared our table for us were it not for the presence of the enemy? God's love gifts sometimes come to his people amid things that cause them heartache and pain, but they can say, 'It is good for me that I was afflicted' (Ps. 119:71). God does his best for his people in every circumstance.

Our enemies, who thought that these hard things would be the end of us, just watch and look on as we emerge from God's table fitter than we ever were before. When Daniel and his friends in Babylon refused to eat the provision of the king of Babylon, they were tested as to their strength and fitness. The Bible says that Daniel and his friends 'were better in appearance and fatter in flesh than all the youths who ate the king's food' (Dan. 1:15). So it is with Christ's people: they emerge from the most difficult providences more healthy than they could ever otherwise have become.

This Shepherd also spreads good things for his people on the table of the gospel. They keep coming back to the gospel, back to his Word and to the same old doctrines of grace. However long it has been since they started following their Shepherd, they never tire of his provision. They have discovered Christ to be their 'bread of life' (John 6:48). So, in a weary world, before a prowling devil and with a wretched heart of unbelief, I can only keep coming back to this great fountain that he opened for sin and uncleanness, whose waters have never run dry and whose streams run sweeter than they have ever been. Can he prepare a table for me in the wilderness (Ps. 78:19)? He already has, and still he says to me, 'Eat, friend, drink, and be drunk with love!'

In the gospel, the Shepherd prepares a table so that he might delight in his people. In 1813, Revd John MacDonald went to Ferintosh in the Scottish Highlands and, in the first month that he was there, his wife died. He was due to preach at the communion season and the elder said, 'You can't preach after your wife has died.' He said, 'I must preach.' The remains of his wife were interred in Ferintosh and MacDonald resumed his duties; and 10,000 people gathered in the open air at Ferintosh for his first communion. He preached on these great words: 'I will betroth you to me for ever' (Hosea 2:19). And, as John Kennedy of Dingwall says, 'Few eyes were tearless in that vast assembly … his soul was lifted on eagle's wings above the sorrow which before depressed him; the widower was lost in the spouse.'[2] Isn't that a marvellous image? 'The widower was lost in the spouse': although he had lost his earthly wife, he delighted in Christ, the great Bridegroom of the church who loves his bride with an everlasting love. In our losses, that is the only place for us to go, too.

David's anointing

David then speaks about another blessing he has enjoyed from God: God has anointed his head with oil. Reading through the Bible, we note from as early as Exodus 29–30 the importance of anointing oil. For example, God required the priests to be anointed as a sign of their consecration: 'You shall take the anointing oil and pour it on his head and anoint him' (Exod.

29:7). Nor would just any oil do—this had to be specially made and blended, and was itself holy. The recipe for producing it was carefully given by God, who then said,

> This shall be my holy anointing oil throughout your generations. It shall not be poured on the body of an ordinary person, and you shall make no other like it in composition. It is holy, and it shall be holy to you. Whoever compounds any like it or whoever puts any of it on an outsider shall be cut off from his people.
>
> (Exod. 30:31–33)

I wonder if David was reflecting on the moment when he was anointed as king over Israel. The story of David begins with God's commission to Samuel to go to Bethlehem to anoint a new king: 'The LORD said to Samuel, "How long will you grieve over Saul, since I have rejected him from being king over Israel? Fill your horn with oil, and go. I will send you to Jesse the Bethlehemite, for I have provided for myself a king among his sons"' (1 Sam. 16:1). There in Bethlehem, notwithstanding the fact that his brothers looked more regal and kingly than he did, David was set apart as king through the act of anointing: 'Samuel took the horn of oil and anointed him in the midst of his brothers. And the Spirit of the LORD rushed upon David from that day forward' (1 Sam. 16:13). The fact was highlighted in Psalm 89:20–21: 'I have found David, my servant; with my holy oil I have anointed him, so that my hand shall be established with him; my arm also shall strengthen him.'

The oil symbolized God's setting David apart as his servant

and the reality of his presence with him, enabling him to fulfil his calling and undertaking to protect him as he did so. That is why Ahithophel's plot against him failed: David was marked out by God. He was protected by a power greater than that of his enemies. So now, as he says, 'You anoint my head with oil', he comforts himself in the presence of his enemies by recalling that he is set apart by a special anointing.

In the Bible, the Hebrew word from which 'anoint' comes also gives us the word 'Messiah' and its Greek equivalent, 'Christ'. We can speak of the messianic theme of the Bible: the anticipation of God's anointed one, who would save his people. Indeed, the New Testament explicitly tells us that the gospel focuses on the anointed Jesus. Here, for example, is the account of Peter preaching the gospel to the Gentiles:

> So Peter opened his mouth and said: 'Truly I understand that God shows no partiality, but in every nation anyone who fears him and does what is right is acceptable to him. As for the word that he sent to Israel, preaching good news of peace through Jesus Christ (he is Lord of all), you yourselves know what happened throughout all Judea, beginning from Galilee after the baptism that John proclaimed: how God anointed Jesus of Nazareth with the Holy Spirit and with power. He went about doing good and healing all who were oppressed by the devil, for God was with him. And we are witnesses of all that he did both in the country of the Jews and in Jerusalem. They put him to death by

hanging him on a tree, but God raised him on the third day and caused him to appear, not to all the people but to us who had been chosen by God as witnesses, who ate and drank with him after he rose from the dead. And he commanded us to preach to the people and to testify that he is the one appointed by God to be judge of the living and the dead. To him all the prophets bear witness that everyone who believes in him receives forgiveness of sins through his name.'

(Acts 10:34–43)

God's anointed one is God's appointed one; set apart and empowered to be Saviour, Jesus now awaits the day when he will sit in judgement over the whole world. No enemy will triumph against the one God has 'Christed', or anointed. Our salvation is according to God's eternal plan, in which God the Father anointed God the Son with God the Holy Spirit. Jesus was empowered and protected, healing the sick and ultimately destroying death.

Wonderfully, this is the same language the New Testament uses of the church, witnessing for Christ in a hostile and cruel world. John says in his letter, 'I write these things to you about those who are trying to deceive you. But the anointing that you received from him abides in you, and you have no need that anyone should teach you. But as his anointing teaches you about everything—and is true, and is no lie, just as it has taught you—abide in him' (1 John 2:26–27). Like David, the early disciples had enemies, who were attempting to deceive and destroy God's people. But John's encouragement is that God's people have an anointing. They are kept in the power and truth of the gospel.

So this is our hope: we have been 'Christed'. The Holy Spirit has been given to us, and we are set apart by him to be servants of God. This is the pledge that God will keep us and guard us every step of the way. We are marked out as belonging to God, and he will not forsake the work of his own hands, even when we walk through trouble (Ps. 138:7–8).

David's cup

If all of this is true—if God is preparing a table for us in the wilderness, consecrating us to himself and guarding us each step of the way—how can we not say, 'my cup overflows'? Our cup is so full of blessing that it can hold no more.

Perhaps we do not feel as though our cup is spilling over. Perhaps we feel more like Naomi, when she said, 'Do not call me Naomi ["pleasant"]; call me Mara ["bitter"], for the Almighty has dealt very bitterly with me. I went away full, and the LORD has brought me back empty' (Ruth 1:20–21). Perhaps, like her, we feel that we have only lost blessings instead of gaining them.

Yet, if there is one good thing about an empty cup, it is that it can be filled again. In fact, the cup of the believer is actually full of all spiritual blessings in heavenly places in Jesus Christ (Eph. 2:6); there is nothing we need that he does not supply, and there is nothing we could ever want that he is not able to provide.

The only reason why that is so is because of the cup Jesus took—a cup that was overflowing, not with the *blessings* but with the *curse* of the covenant. To contemplate drinking it made him stagger; the sorrow in his soul translated into blood dripping through his skin. 'My Father,' he said, 'if it be possible, let this cup pass from me' (Matt. 26:39). But if his people were to be redeemed and saved—if they were to enjoy a cup brimful of blessing—it was not possible for Jesus to forego his cup, so he willingly took it. His cup overflowed with the judgement of God upon sin; he drank it and emptied it. The result for us is glorious; we can say that 'The LORD is my chosen portion and my cup' (Ps. 16:5). We shall never experience the forsakenness of Calvary; but because of the One who did, our cup can overflow with blessings, even though our lot may sometimes be a hard one.

And, if your cup overflows, make sure it overflows into someone else's cup. Make sure you tell of what God has done for your soul and of the satisfaction you have found in Jesus. Share the news of your satisfaction and completeness in him. Even if, like Naomi, you have tasted Mara's bitter waters and your cup seems more empty than full, never forget the source of the stream. There is still a clear river of water of life proceeding from the throne of God and of the Lamb (Rev. 22:1), and it can run right down into your cup and make it spill over with blessing.

Have you discovered such joy and satisfaction in Christ that you would gladly have the wilderness, the dark valley, the enemies, the difficult providences, and the sense of unworthiness and emptiness, just to have him fill your cup and bless your soul? Do you know his anointing? Do you feast at his table? Are you resting in him, drawing from him, satisfied with him? Are you complete in Christ, the fountain that never runs dry?

Reflect on these points

1. *The moment you belong to the flock of God, you will have enemies. If you are a Christian, the devil is your enemy. The world itself can be your enemy; its godlessness, secularism, self-interest and pleasure-seeking lifestyle are all the enemies of the flock of Jesus Christ. Our own sinful natures are our greatest enemy.*

2. *God so overrules the events of our lives that the table of his providence has good things for us to enjoy. They may not always be easy or pleasant things, but they are good. Even when God sends difficult things our way, he works them for our good. Is it not the case that the things that have influenced us most are not those that we chose for ourselves but those that we did not choose?*

3. *If your cup overflows, make sure it overflows into someone else's cup. Make sure you tell of what God has done for your soul and of the satisfaction you have found in Jesus. Share the news of your satisfaction and completeness in him.*

Dwelling in the Shepherd's house

Surely goodness and mercy shall follow me all the days of my life, and I shall dwell in the house of the LORD for ever.

(v. 6)

By any standard, this is a remarkable and glorious conclusion to a remarkable and glorious psalm. In the psalm, David has been expressing the relationship between himself and his God in terms of the relationship between a shepherd and his sheep. He has also been talking about the different experiences that he has faced in life: through them all, he has been conscious of the constant presence of the Shepherd with him. His final gaze is very much into the future.

This verse tells us several things. It tells us about how David regarded his own life and existence. It also tells us about how David viewed God: his Shepherd had been providing and would continue to provide for him right to the very end of his life. But then it tells us about David's great hope: that one day he would come into God's house and be there for ever.

David's perspectives

A perspective is just a way of looking at something. If you sit in the same seat in church for many years, you have your own unique perspective on the building and what it looks like. If you arrive in church one Sunday and someone else is in 'your' seat, you are displaced and suddenly the building looks slightly different. You have a different perspective.

It is the same with life: we can have different perspectives on our lives. David has two different perspectives on his life and they are summarized in two phrases in verse 6. He talks on the one hand about 'all the days of his life', clearly referring to his life here in this world. He is thinking about today, tomorrow, and all the days that stretch out into the unknown future of his life to the very end of it in this world.

But then he has another perspective, because the very last Hebrew phrase of this psalm is translated into English as 'for ever'. David has this twofold view of his existence. He wants to talk about things that are true of him now, and he also wants to talk about the 'for ever', about life beyond this one. He wants to stretch his horizon beyond the space-time world that he inhabits at present and think about glorious things in the future. He anticipates going to be with the Shepherd in the Shepherd's house for ever.

I think it is important to labour this point. Too few people have these perspectives on their lives. Too many people have only one perspective: they live their lives in the here and now and are only concerned about 'all the days of their life' here in this world. These are those described elsewhere in the Psalms as 'men of the world whose portion is in this life' (Ps. 17:14). While it is important to think about our lives here and the priorities we set for them, it is possible to stop there and not think about the 'for ever'.

It is necessary that we capture the perspective that David has because it runs right through the Scriptures. Paul says in 2 Corinthians 4:16–18,

... we do not lose heart. Though our outer nature is

wasting away, our inner nature is being renewed day by day. For this slight momentary affliction is preparing for us an eternal weight of glory beyond all comparison, as we look not to the things that are seen but to the things that are unseen. For the things that are seen are transient, but the things that are unseen are eternal.

To confine our view to the things that are time-bound is to hold onto things that are transient and temporal. If that was all Paul had, he would have had nothing. We want to look at things that are not seen, to look at eternal realities and see our lives through the lens of the Bible; we want the perspective on our lives that God himself has. We need to remember that we are creatures of a moment, yet we are also creatures that will live for ever.

So David ends the psalm by talking of life here, but he knows that life here is not all there is. We dare not live our lives as though this life is all there is. Being a Christian means that we have discovered the reality of these two perspectives, and that we take them with us wherever we go.

David's provisions
David says, 'Surely goodness and mercy shall follow me all the days of my life' [or 'every day of my life']. David summarizes the whole of his life here in this world, where the goodness and mercy of God have been with him, are with him and will be with him. Whatever else may be true of him, this is also true: God's goodness and mercy are with him each day.

Firstly, he speaks of the *goodness* of God. He is aware that God has been good to him every moment, every day and at every turn. God's people in every age and in every generation have discovered this for themselves. In Exodus 33:18–19 we read about a remarkable exchange between Moses and God: 'Moses said, "Please show me your glory." And [God] said, "I will make all my goodness pass before you and will proclaim before you my name 'The LORD'. And I will be gracious to whom I will be gracious, and will show mercy on whom I will show mercy …"'

God allowed Moses to see a little of his glory and said to Moses, 'I will make my *goodness* pass before you.' We cannot know everything about God—to see God's glory is beyond us. There are depths to the being of God that we cannot even begin to measure. But in his grace and in his gospel, God says to us, 'I will show you my goodness.' God's people have seen his goodness and they have discovered that it is abundant. Psalm 31:19–20 expresses it this way:

> Oh, how abundant is your goodness,
>   which you have stored up for those who fear you
> and worked for those who take refuge in you,
>   in the sight of the children of mankind!
> In the cover of your presence you hide them
>   from the plots of men;
> you store them in your shelter
>   from the strife of tongues.

Psalm 65:4 says, 'Blessed is the one you choose and bring near, to dwell in your courts! We shall be satisfied with the goodness of your house, the holiness of your temple!' That is the anthem of the believer, and it is of the essence of the new covenant. Jeremiah, the prophet of the new covenant, tied the blessing of God's goodness with the shepherding care of God over his people:

> Hear the word of the LORD, O nations,
>> and declare it in the coastlands far away;
> say, 'He who scattered Israel will gather him,
>> and will keep him as a shepherd keeps his flock.'
> For the LORD has ransomed Jacob
>> and has redeemed him from hands too strong for him.
> They shall come and sing aloud on the height of Zion,
>> and they shall be radiant over the goodness of the LORD,
> over the grain, the wine, and the oil,
>> and over the young of the flock and the herd;
> their life shall be like a watered garden,
>> and they shall languish no more.
> Then shall the young women rejoice in the dance,
>> and the young men and the old shall be merry.
> I will turn their mourning into joy;
>> I will comfort them, and give them gladness for
>> sorrow.
> I will feast the soul of the priests with abundance,
>> and my people shall be satisfied with my goodness,
>>>> declares the Lord.
>>>>> (Jer. 31:10–14)

The Holy Spirit convicts us of our sin and brings home to us our badness; the gospel then points us to Christ and to the goodness of God. We have discovered very little in ourselves with which we can be satisfied, but we have discovered that God is all goodness; that 'The LORD is good, a stronghold in the day of trouble; he knows those who take refuge in him' (Nahum 1:7). This is the unmistakable emphasis of faith: 'God is good.'

As David reflects on the past and anticipates the future, he knows, as Paul also knew, that God works everything for good in the experience of his people (Rom. 8:28). But he is also aware of the *mercy* of God. The Hebrew word translated 'mercy', *hesed*, speaks of God's commitment to his covenant. This note is picked up in the *Sing Psalms* translation of Psalm 23:

> So surely your covenant mercy and grace
> will follow me closely in all of my ways.[1]

This Hebrew word appears about 250 times in the Old Testament, and over half of these occurrences are in the Psalms. We sing constantly of the mercy of God and we are commanded to do so. Psalm 106:1 says, 'Praise the LORD! Oh give thanks to the LORD, for he is good, for his steadfast love [his mercy, his covenant commitment] endures for ever!'

The psalmist put it like this on one occasion: 'I will rejoice and be glad in your steadfast love, because you have seen my affliction' (Ps. 31:7). David's reason to be glad was not because of his affliction, but because of the covenant faithfulness of his God. That is all that faith needs to lean on. '"For the mountains may depart, and the hills be removed, but my steadfast love [covenant mercy] shall not depart from you, and my covenant of peace shall not be removed," says the LORD, who has compassion on you' (Isa. 54:10).

In our verse, David speaks of the goodness of God—God giving us what we don't deserve—and the mercy of God—God not giving us what we do deserve. The Shepherd is faithful to his covenant promise, and he supplies our every need according to the riches of his glory by Christ Jesus. In his book on Psalm 23, Douglas MacMillan quotes from an old Highland elder whom he heard preaching on one occasion. He suggests that the elder was a better shepherd than a theologian, but says that 'he was wonderful'. And the elder said this on one occasion:

> What do I think of when I think of goodness and mercy? I think of the fellows taking the sheep home, walking down the road there with their sticks. The sheep are coming behind them and, behind the sheep, are the two dogs, one is called goodness and the other is called mercy. You watch them. Sheep being what they are when the shepherd's back is turned, they will try and sneak off the road. You see a sheep on one side and off it goes trying to get back to the pasture and the mountains without even the shepherd whistling; what happens—Goodness runs out and circles the sheep and turns it back into the flock and into the path of God. Then a little further along the road another one will do

the same or two or three will do it and there you will see
Mercy running out and turning the sheep back too. Ah
they are two lovely sheepdogs, Goodness and Mercy.[2]

Isn't that a beautiful illustration? If the Lord is truly our
Shepherd, we are trying to follow him; yet often we have
strayed from the path that we should have been walking. On
these occasions, it has taken his two sheepdogs, Goodness and
Mercy, to run out, encircle us and bring us back.

When David says 'goodness and mercy shall *follow me*', he is
actually using a very strong Hebrew word that means to 'chase'
or 'pursue'. The image is that, wherever the Shepherd takes the
flock, goodness and mercy are pursuing the sheep. This is how
Eugene Peterson translates the phrase in *The Message*: 'Your
beauty and love *chase after me* every day of my life.'

Goodness and mercy don't let the flock out of sight. From
this psalm emerges this beautiful picture of the flock moving
along the road with the Shepherd leading and goodness and
mercy following. The flock is constantly surrounded by the
shepherding covenant care of God. Those who belong to the
flock of Jesus don't keep their eye on goodness and mercy but
on the Shepherd. As they do so, wherever he goes, they go; and
wherever he leads his flock, goodness and mercy chase after
the flock.

I suspect that there are many people who want to reverse
that order; who want to keep their eyes on goodness and
mercy, fill their lives with good and easy things and be
constantly aware of enjoying the many blessings God has to

give. If everything is going well, they conclude that God is indeed their Shepherd.

But the order of the psalm is different. It is the Shepherd who goes out ahead, and it is upon him that we must keep our attention. If we are to know goodness and mercy following us, we must first look to Christ's leading. Keep your eye on him, not on the benefits he brings. If you do so, he will lead you into places where you will be pursued by his goodness and mercy every day of your life.

Hugh Martin, in his great book on the Holy Spirit, *The Abiding Presence*, says, 'You do not deal with reminiscences of Christ; memories and mementos of Him, however accurate; conceptions, notions, ideas concerning him, however true; no, nor even with mere doctrines concerning Him, however truly divine and infinitely precious in their own place as these unquestionably are. You deal with him, and he with you.'[3] That is the secret of living the Christian life. You run your race with patience, looking to Jesus (Heb. 12:1–2). Keep your eye on the Shepherd and let him lead you. As you follow, goodness and mercy will pursue you and will never let you go.

If we wish to have the assurance of sins forgiven and peace with God, and to know that we have the blessing and favour of heaven, we need to lift up our eyes to Jesus, not to the blessings he confers. If we are looking for peace in our souls, we do not look to peace, we look to Jesus. If we are looking for fulfilment, happiness and contentment, we do not pursue these things, we pursue Jesus. If we follow him, goodness and mercy will pursue us all our days.

David's prospects

But what about when 'all the days of my life' are ended? What about beyond this life? David's ultimate prospect is this: 'I shall dwell in the house of the LORD for ever.' The phrase 'the house of the LORD' is used often in the Old Testament to refer to the temple. The book of Psalms often uses it in this way, such as at Psalm 122:1: 'I was glad when they said to me, "Let us go to the house of the LORD!"' But the temple was only a passing shadow that anticipated something greater. When John saw into heaven, he said there was no temple there (Rev. 21:22). There was no physical building which one could identify as the house of the Lord. The reason? The Lamb was the temple. Heaven is the house of the Lord and it is filled with the glory of Jesus Christ. Heaven is where God dwells with his people and they with him. It is where goodness dissolves into glory, as Jesus brings all his people at last into the glory of his presence.

What a way for this great psalm to end! It is not a long psalm, but it takes us into the longest of all visions and lifts our eyes to the most glorious of all horizons. David says to us that those who belong to the flock of Jesus know that they will dwell in God's house for ever.

This psalm has been all about movement—lying down, rising up, travelling, being led, walking through the valley of the shadow of death. But David's ultimate hope is the prospect of rest. He anticipates *dwelling*; he looks forward to being in a place from which he will never be asked to move. Many times along the pilgrimage his Shepherd took him through difficult and dark places and he longed for the Shepherd to move him on. Now, however, he anticipates the ultimate glory of resting and of staying in God's house.

The shadows of separation fall over every blessing we enjoy here; the fellowship between disciples is always marred by the words 'Rise, let us go from here' (John 14:31). Now, however, David says, 'I am going to *dwell*; I am going to *stay* in the house of the Lord, and he will never again say to me, "Rise, let us go from here."' This psalm has been talking about different places: difficult places, the valley of the shadow, green pastures, still waters; but David's hope is the final place he has in view—the house of the Lord.

He has been talking about the Shepherd's presence with him, about God with him in this world; but his prospect is that he will dwell with God in a better world. The *promise* of the covenant is that God is with his people here; but the *prospect* of the covenant is that they will be with him there. The Word became flesh and dwelt among us (John 1:14), but only for a greater end—that we might be with Christ at last. The glory of the gospel is that Jesus came from heaven to earth; but the hope of the gospel is that he will bring his people from earth to heaven.

This psalm has been talking about exposure to enemies round about, looking on, watching and waiting; but it closes on this great note of eternal security, when God will shut all his people in and all his enemies out. It makes all the difference in the world which side of that closed door we are on when he comes again. But it is not until we can say 'The Lord is my Shepherd' that we can ever say, 'I will dwell in the house of the Lord for ever'. We need for ever to lose the idea that we can have the prospect of heaven with Christ without being committed to him in a saving relationship of faith here in this world.

On the other hand, all those who are able to say 'Yes, he is my Shepherd'—whatever they say about their pilgrimage and however they describe the ways that he leads them—will say with David, 'He will take me home.' We can have this great assurance that, when the earthly house of this tabernacle is dissolved and vanishes away for ever, we will have a building of God, a house not made with hands, eternal in the heavens (2 Cor. 5:1). The green pastures were good, but they were not home. The still waters were good, but they were not home. The valley was not home.

Maybe the green pastures gave us a longing for home. Maybe the still waters enabled us to taste the sweetness of home. The valley caused us to groan with longing for home. While this psalm is a beautiful psalm, it is a psalm of exile, written far from home with the longing that one day the Shepherd will take his sheep home.

One of my most abiding memories from childhood is of when I would help my grandfather take the sheep from the moor to the croft and we would walk what seemed to be miles into nowhere to get the sheep and bring them home. They would come off the moor and round to the back of my grandfather's croft, and I still remember being awestruck at seeing those sheep recognize his gate. They passed every other gate, but knew when they were home; then they would follow that well-trodden path. Time after time, they would simply stop at that gate and wait for it to be opened, and then they would come on to the croft and be home.

But I never saw my grandfather take the flock right into his house. His sheep knew they were home, but they were never *in* his home. That is the prospect of this psalm: 'The LORD is my shepherd ... and I shall dwell in the house of the LORD.' He is not just going to take his sheep home; he is going to take them *into his home*.

And when he takes his flock into his home, he is going to turn around, and, for the very first time, they are going to see their Shepherd's face. Here we see through a glass darkly. Here he is leading—that means there is a sense in which his back is to us. We are simply following him, walking by faith and not by sight. But then we shall see face to face (1 Cor. 13:12). The flock will see his face and his name will be on their foreheads (Rev. 22:4). They will bow before him and will sing, 'The Lord is my Shepherd.' See how Anne Ross Cousins expressed it in her hymn 'Immanuel's Land':

> With mercy and with judgement my web
>   of time he wove,

And aye, the dews of sorrow were lustred
    with his love;
I'll bless the hand that guided, I'll
    bless the heart that planned
When throned where glory dwelleth
    in Immanuel's land …

They've summoned me before them, but there
    I may not come,
My Lord says, 'Come up hither', my Lord says,
    'Welcome home!'
My kingly King, at his white throne, my presence
    doth command
Where glory, glory dwelleth in
    Immanuel's land.

We can all sing Psalm 23. But *may* we sing it? Do we belong to his flock? Is our trust in his saving power? Is our faith in his irresistible Word? Is our confidence in his keeping grace? If so, keep singing that psalm. A day is coming when he is going to divide his sheep from all others; it makes all the difference in the world, and for eternity, whether or not we can truly say of God in Christ, 'my Shepherd', and whether he will truly say of us, 'my sheep'. For it is to his sheep alone that he will say at the end, 'Come, you who are blessed by my Father, inherit the kingdom prepared for you from the foundation of the world' (Matt. 25:34).

Reflect on these points

1. To confine our view to the things that are time-bound is to hold onto things that are transient and temporal. We want to look at things that are not seen, to look at eternal realities; we want the perspective on our lives that God himself has.

2. If the Lord is truly our Shepherd, we are trying to follow him; yet often we have strayed from the path that we should have been walking. On these occasions, it has taken his two sheepdogs, Goodness and Mercy, to run out, encircle us and bring us back.

3. Many people want to keep their eyes on goodness and mercy, fill their lives with good things and be constantly aware of enjoying the many blessings God has to give. If everything is going well, they conclude that God is indeed their Shepherd. But the order of the psalm is different. It is upon the Shepherd that we must keep our attention. Keep your eye on him, not on the benefits he brings.

4. Maybe the green pastures gave us a longing for home. Maybe the still waters enabled us to taste the sweetness of home. The valley caused us to groan with longing for home. One day the Shepherd will take his sheep home.

5. Here he is leading—his back is to us. We are simply following him, walking by faith and not by sight. But then we shall see face to face. The flock will see his face and his name will be on their foreheads.

Two metrical versions of Psalm 23

Both of these can be found in *Sing Psalms: New Metrical Versions of the Book of Psalms with The Scottish Psalter* (Free Church of Scotland, 2004).

Psalm 23   C.M.

> The LORD's my shepherd, I'll not want.
>   He makes me down to lie
> In pastures green: he leadeth me
>   the quiet waters by.
> My soul he doth restore again;
>   and me to walk doth make
> Within the paths of righteousness,
>   ev'n for his own name's sake.
> Yea, though I walk in death's dark vale,
>   yet will I fear none ill:
> For thou art with me; and thy rod
>   and staff me comfort still.
> My table thou hast furnishèd
>   in presence of my foes;
> My head thou dost with oil anoint,
>   and my cup overflows.
> Goodness and mercy all my life
>   shall surely follow me:
> And in GOD's house for evermore
>   my dwelling-place shall be.

(The Scottish Psalter, 1560)

Psalm 23   11 11 11

The LORD is my shepherd; no want shall I know.
He makes me lie down where the green pastures grow;
He leads me to rest where the calm waters flow.
My wandering steps he brings back to his way,
In straight paths of righteousness making me stay;
And this he has done his great name to display.
Though I walk in death's valley, where darkness is near,
Because you are with me, no evil I'll fear;
Your rod and your staff bring me comfort and cheer.
In the sight of my en'mies a table you spread.
The oil of rejoicing you pour on my head;
My cup overflows and I'm graciously fed.
So surely your covenant mercy and grace
Will follow me closely in all of my ways;
I will dwell in the house of the LORD all my days.

(Sing Psalms, 2004)

Endnotes

Ch. 1 Knowing the Shepherd personally

1   Robert Frost, 'The Road Not Taken'.

Ch. 2 Following the Shepherd's directions

1   Frances J. Crosby, 'He Hideth my Soul'.

2   Douglas MacMillan, *The Lord My Shepherd* (Bridgend: Bryntirion, 2004), pp. 84–89.

Ch. 4 Enjoying the Shepherd's protection

1   George Adam Smith, *Historical Geography of the Holy Land* (London: Hodder and Stoughton, 1896), p. 311.

2   John Calvin, *Institutes of the Christian Religion* (Louisville, KY: Westminster John Knox Press, 2006), 1:17:10.

3   Robert Murray McCheyne, 'Jehovah Tsidkenu' ('The Lord our Righteousness').

Ch. 5 Trusting in the Shepherd's provision

1   These words are quoted and explained in the context of William Cowper's life and ministry in Faith Cook's excellent work *Our Hymn-Writers and their Hymns* (Darlington: Evangelical Press, 2005), pp. 213–242.

2   John Kennedy, *The Apostle of the North* (Glasgow: Free Presbyterian Publications, 1978), p. 47.

Ch. 6 Dwelling in the Shepherd's house

1   *Sing Psalms* (Edinburgh: Free Church of Scotland, 2004).

2   MacMillan, *The Lord My Shepherd*, pp. 120–121.

3   Hugh Martin, *The Abiding Presence* (Edinburgh: Knox Press [n.d.]), p. 37.

Also available

When God makes streams in the desert
Revival blessings in the Bible

ROGER ELLSWORTH

128PP, PAPERBACK

ISBN 978-1-84625-176-4

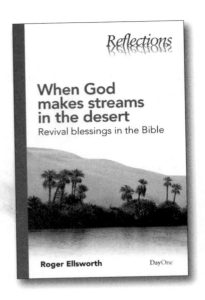

What is biblical revival? Many Christians associate revival with special meetings that used to take place once or twice a year. Guest preachers and singers would be brought in, and special evening services were designed to encourage believers to get closer to the Lord and to convince unbelievers to accept him as their Saviour.

But that is not revival. Biblical revival is about God bringing his people back to spiritual vitality. Only Christians can be revived because only they have spiritual life, having been regenerated by the Spirit of God on the basis of the redeeming work of Christ.

Learn what the Bible teaches about revival, and be inspired to pray that, even in our day, God will make streams flow in the desert!

'With a relentless focus on the Bible itself, Roger Ellsworth reminds us that true revival is a sovereign work of God that radically affects our lives. The best recommendation I can give of this book is that it made me long more intensely and pray more fervently for God to act in the midst of his people.'
CHAD DAVIS, PASTOR, GRACE COMMUNITY CHURCH, MARTIN, TENNESSEE, USA

'When God Makes Streams in the Desert reminds us that revival is present when, as Brian Edwards says, 'remarkable life and power that cannot be explained adequately in any human terms' moves into our churches and causes us to do what we do 'at a different level'. This book will change the way you think about and pray for revival.'
PAUL ORRICK, PASTOR, FIRST BAPTIST CHURCH, GREENVILLE, OHIO, USA

On wings of prayer
Praying the ACTS way

REGGIE WEEMS

112PP, PAPERBACK

ISBN 978-1-84625-178-8

Constructing a prayer life is often like putting a puzzle together without the box's cover. Having a picture makes all the difference. Bible prayers create a model of what prayer can be; exciting, fulfilling and powerful. Using a simple acrostic makes prayer memorable, interesting and focused. You too can learn to pray following this simple outline utilized by men and women who experience the transforming power of prayer.

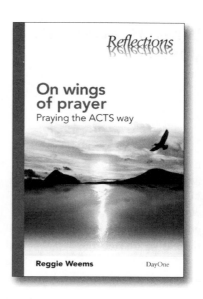

'This brief work on prayer will encourage you to pray, teach you to pray, and give you precious gems about prayer along the way. It taught me things I did not know, and reminded me of things I had forgotten.'
PAUL DAVID WASHER, HEARTCRY MISSIONARY SOCIETY

'Because of the unique nature of the Christian discipline of prayer, most books on prayer are more inspiring than they are helpful. Pastor Reggie Weems has achieved what only a few have ever done in Christian history. This book is orthodox, penetrating, motivating and inspiring, all in one slender, readable volume. If you are hoping to enhance your walk with the Master, here is one book that will bless your soul.'
PAIGE PATTERSON, PRESIDENT, SOUTHWESTERN BAPTIST THEOLOGICAL SEMINARY, FORT WORTH, TEXAS, USA

When Heaven calls your name

People in the Bible who heard God speak

ROGER ELLSWORTH

128PP, PAPERBACK

ISBN 978-1-84625-102-3

Believing that repetition indicates emphasis, Roger Ellsworth examines occasions in the Bible in which God the Father or God the Son repeated someone's name. He asserts that these instances were meant to make certain truths 'dance' before our eyes. In an increasingly difficult and challenging world, these truths will thrill, comfort and guide all those who genuinely embrace them.

'God speaks. He has spoken, and he continues to speak today. Through these vivid portraits of Heaven's calls, you will overhear the voice of God speaking specifically and clearly to you.'
TODD BRADY, PASTOR OF THE FIRST BAPTIST CHURCH OF PADUCAH, KENTUCKY, USA

'Roger Ellsworth has given us another book full of pastoral integrity and fidelity to the Word of God. *When Heaven calls your name* is both exegetically sound and devotionally warm—a book that is as heart-stirring as it is instructional. The readers of this book who hear their names called will grow in the faith and knowledge of our Lord and Saviour, Jesus Christ. I heartily recommend it!'
IVAN SCHOEN, PASTOR, MARANATHA BAPTIST CHURCH, POPLAR GROVE, ILLINOIS, USA

Under God's smile
The Trinitarian Blessing of 2 Corinthians 13:14

DEREK PRIME

128PP, PAPERBACK

ISBN 978-1-84625-059-0

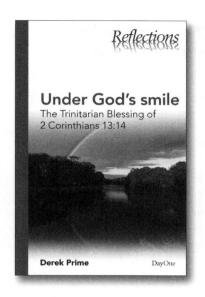

During recent decades, it has become the practice of Christians in many churches and in university and college Christian Unions to commit one another to God's grace and care with the words 'May the grace of the Lord Jesus Christ, and the love of God, and the fellowship of the Holy Spirit be with us all' (2 Corinthians 13:14). They are familiar words, but what do they actually mean? For what are we praying?

So that we do not repeat these words without appreciating their full implication, Derek Prime explores them and considers the three Persons of the Trinity in their different, yet perfectly harmonious, relationship to every believer. Written in an easy-to-read style, this book is thoroughly rooted in the Scriptures and is a demonstration that solid biblical truth is both heart-warming and exciting.

'Wholesome food for the average Christian reader and devotional writing of the highest order'
EVANGELICALS NOW

'An easily-read book, helpful in all stages of Christian life'
GRACE MAGAZINE

'Derek Prime's ministry is much appreciated by many Christian groups, including ourselves. Like all his other books ... biblically based and easy to read'
ASSOCIATED PRESBYTERIANS NEWS

'If, like me, you are constantly on the lookout for books that say a great deal in short order, you will be delighted by what you hold in your hand. It is a special gift not only to expound what the blessing of the triune God means, but also to explain why it matters. We have come to expect this from Derek Prime, and once again he hits the mark.'
ALISTAIR BEGG, SENIOR PASTOR, PARKSIDE CHURCH, CHAGRIN FALLS, OHIO

They echoed the voice of God

Reflections on the Minor Prophets

ROGER ELLSWORTH

128PP, PAPERBACK

ISBN 978-1-84625-101-6

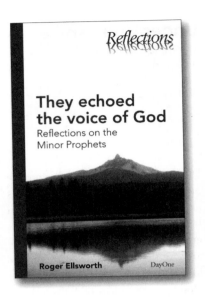

Many carry a little Bible and believe in a little God. Their Bibles are little because they ignore so many of its books. Their God is little because they ignore so many of the Bible's truths. The Minor Prophets can help us. These men made sense of their circumstances and found strength for their challenges by basking in the God who was above it all and in it all. The God they served was wise enough to plan and strong enough to achieve. This study of their messages will help us have both bigger Bibles and a bigger God.

'Roger Ellsworth helps us appreciate how the so-called Minor Prophets make known the character and work of our great God. This book is a great introduction to and overview of their prophecies. Read it to become acquainted with these sometimes overlooked servants and, more importantly, with the unchangeable God whose message they proclaimed.'
TOM ASCOL, DIRECTOR OF FOUNDERS MINISTRIES AND PASTOR, GRACE BAPTIST CHURCH, CAPE CORAL, FLORIDA

'Laced with helpful, practical application, this book shows how each prophet emphasized a particular aspect of God's character, giving an overall picture that is compelling.'
JIM WINTER, MINISTER OF HORSELL EVANGELICAL CHURCH, WOKING